This Is Me, Is That You?

THIS IS ME,
IS THAT YOU?

ENCOUNTERS WITH
SCHIZOPHRENIA

● ● ●

STEVEN POSER

Yale
UNIVERSITY PRESS
New Haven and London

Published with assistance from the foundation established in memory of
Calvin Chapin of the Class of 1788, Yale College.

Yale University Press books may be purchased in quantity for educational,
business, or promotional use. For information, please e-mail sales.
press@yale.edu (U.S. office) or sales@yaleup.co.uk (U.K. office).

Set in Adobe Garamond Pro type by IDS Infotech Ltd.
Printed in the United States of America.

ISBN 978-0-300-27654-1 (hardcover : alk. paper)
Library of Congress Control Number: 2024944719
A catalogue record for this book is available from the British Library.

This paper meets the requirements of ANSI/NISO Z39.48-1992
(Permanence of Paper).

10 9 8 7 6 5 4 3 2 1

Contents

Acknowledgments

This book owes a great deal to the early encouragement and continued support of Christopher Bollas over the long course of its gestation.

During the years of my psychoanalytic training, I was taught, mentored, and supervised by two outstanding clinicians, Phyllis Meadow and Murray H. Sherman, who took me under their wings and, by their example, introduced me to the very idea of doing psychotherapeutic work with schizophrenic patients.

At the "Wingfield Asylum for the Insane," "Dr. Harold Hartman" and "Dr. Walter Peterson" welcomed me into their extraordinary domain and entrusted me to engage with the women who are the subject of this book.

In more recent years, I thank my colleagues and friends in the Faculty Psychotherapy Conference of the Department of Psychiatry, Mt. Sinai Hospital, New York. Over the past ten years, I have presented to this group each of the three women portrayed here. I couldn't have asked for a more insightful and illuminating audience to get a sense of how this unusual clinical material was coming across.

The freelance editor Jonas Goodman was instrumental in my transforming a sprawling 400-page clinical diary into the three-part structure of half that length it is today. That radical revision, plus his patient, wise management of my writing process at the time, made this a very different, and, I think, better book than it was before.

At Yale University Press, Jessie Kindig led me through the final stages of revision with consummate grace and skill. I feel very lucky to have found such a thoughtful and sensitive editor to shepherd this book into the world.

My greatest debt is to "Agnes," "Mrs. Lutzky," and "Lucia," for their willingness to admit me into their uniquely personal realities. For this privilege, I have no words to express the depth of my feeling for what each of them has given me.

Note to the Reader

Though I have chosen a literary form, style, and structure to bring the women of this book to life, it is a work of nonfiction. All events are actual, recreated to the best of my recollection. Conversations, however, are approximate, reconstructed based on notes I compiled at the time to convey the substance, mood, and tone of actual dialogues. Several scenes in this book represent a composite and compression of events, and although each of these women represents a real patient with whom I interacted, I have gone to such significant lengths to alter their identities, recollections, and histories that, as portrayed here, they have no counterparts in the real world. All names have been entirely changed to abide by the medical ethic of preserving the confidentiality of patients and that of their families. I have also disguised the identities of all other characters appearing in this book, including the professional staff and the institution itself.

This Is Me, Is That You?

Prologue

In the spring of 1994, as part of my training to become a psychoanalyst, I applied for a clinical internship in one of the last remaining nineteenth-century mental hospitals in New England, here called the "Wingfield Asylum for the Insane." This was not a typical route into the profession, but I had some very specific reasons for wanting to do it. As it happened, I had been analyzed, trained, and supervised by clinicians who had all worked with patients suffering from the uncanny condition known as schizophrenia and were devoted to understanding this most devastating form of mental illness. I thought that I might be well suited to this kind of work, given my eclectic background in academic philosophy and the world of contemporary art. I had recently immersed myself in the origin myths and religious life of tribal peoples, particularly those of Aboriginal Australia and New Guinea. I had a fascination with people living in realms of subjective experience, other realities, radically different from my own. Instead of feeling threatened, horrified, appalled, or helpless in the face of those who had truly "lost their minds," the prospect seemed to me a great privilege, an opportunity to explore the human psyche in some of its most extreme and enigmatic states of disorder.

I was fortunate in that the director of psychology at Wingfield, Dr. Harold Hartman, had also been trained as a psychoanalyst. This made him especially sympathetic to my wish to be allowed to sit with chronically ill patients and just listen to them talk. I wanted to understand what was going on in their minds and, in accordance with a fundamental premise of psychoanalysis, I believed that the best way of doing that was to let the patient speak freely and at length, without imposing any preconceived agenda of my own. Dr. Hartman liked my background in art and the humanities, as well as the special emphasis in my training on working with schizophrenic patients. He told me that when he first came to Wingfield many years ago, that was just what he did—sat himself down in every single ward in the hospital and let the patients make themselves known to him, or not, each in their own way. He said that he couldn't pay me for anything I did while I was there, but that he did have something to offer that he thought I might like. Then he reached into his desk and gave me the heavy, old-fashioned key to a locked ward of some three dozen middle-aged women located in Haddon House, a building set apart from the others and devoted to the most regressed, chronically ill patients in the entire hospital complex. I stayed on the ward for two years, spending one full day a week, primarily in the dayroom, a large common area looking out on bucolic greenery, where, over time, I was able to enter into ongoing conversations with three of these women—"Agnes," "Mrs. Lutzky," and "Lucia." This book tells the story of my coming to know each of them from the first day to the last, two years that remain indelible in my mind and which marked a turning point in my life.

"Agnes," "Mrs. Lutzky," and "Lucia," are, of course, not their real names. I named Agnes, a middle-aged woman who spoke in the high-pitched, excited voice of a nursery school child, after *Agnus Dei,* the Lamb of God. I named Mrs. Lutzky, a Jewish woman who had grown up in New York, after the accountant who, many years ago, kept the books for my father's diamond cutting workshop, which was located in a grimy old building in Manhattan's diamond district. Lucia, with whom I formed a particularly moving connection, was named after James Joyce's daughter, who also had a psychotic breakdown in her early years and spent the greater part of her adult life in mental hospitals. Each of these women represents a real patient with whom I interacted; however, I have gone to such significant lengths to disguise anything that might disclose their true identities that "Agnes," "Mrs. Lutzky," and "Lucia" exist only in the pages of this book and have no counterparts in the real world. I have also changed the names of all other patients, the staff, the institution and its buildings, and any other identifying references to protect these women's anonymity and that of their families.

Most of the patients on the ward had been institutionalized for several decades with no readily foreseeable end, barring death—which many of them claimed had already happened to them long ago. They suffered unremitting hallucinations and delusions. Some were completely withdrawn into speechless isolation. After many previous hospitalizations and the failure of every form of treatment known to psychiatry, they were regarded as irretrievably lost to their illness. If they had responded reasonably well to any of the psychotropic drugs that, beginning in the 1950s, had become the standard of care for psychotic disorders, they might have been discharged "into the community" or given refuge in a group home. But no amount of antipsychotic medication relieved them of their symptoms. Had they had access to intensive psychotherapy at the first onset on their illness, they might have had a better chance of recovery. But that was long ago, and it seems never to have happened, leaving very little prospect of their ever returning to a life outside the hospital.

Over the two years that I was on the ward, I observed occasional visits by the parents or relatives of a few of the patients. Family members took them out in the morning and returned them to the ward later in the afternoon. There did not seem to be the financial, community, or familial resources available to do any more than this. Confinement to what was known as the "Continuing Treatment Unit" was the last resort, the place patients were sent when all else failed and there was nowhere else for them to go.

These years, the mid-1990s, were the tail end of a now-lost era in the long-term care of the mentally ill. Since then, and starting already in the 1970s, most of these formerly grand and idealistic care facilities, these total environments for living, have disappeared. Wingfield no longer exists, having been shut down many years ago, its elegant Victorian buildings demolished and replaced by a shopping mall. The reasons for this have to do with the evolution of psychiatric medicine. Beginning in the 1950s, anti-psychotic drugs had proved effective for many patients in reducing the hallucinations and delusions of acute psychosis and preventing relapse. There has consequently been a progressive movement to close down old-fashioned mental hospitals like Wingfield, and "de-institutionalize" patients into community-based care. Most people diagnosed with schizophrenia today receive their psychiatric care in public hospitals, day programs, and clinics. Their treatment is dominated by a drug regimen overseen by a medically trained psychiatrist, with support from other mental health professionals, such as clinical psychologists, social workers, and psychiatric nurses.

Corresponding to this movement is the prevailing view in the medical community that schizophrenia is fundamentally a progressively disabling brain disease with no known cause or cure. There are no physiological, neurological, or genetic tests to determine whether someone has this disease. Diagnosis is made by observing whether a person is hearing voices or seeing things that aren't there, has delusional ideas about who they are or what's going on in the world around them, or whose speech has become disorganized or incoherent. Medication is understood as contributing to the management and mitigation of these symptoms as best as possible in each case. The end result of this view is a general pessimism about such patients ever getting better. It means that people living in a chronic state of psychosis, like those I observed at Wingfield, who failed to respond to any form of treatment for a very long time, were likely to remain severely disabled for the rest of their lives.

Nowadays, it is widely recognized that patients diagnosed with schizophrenia are suffering from a complex disorder that transcends the purely medical model of disease, a disorder that involves not only biological but also psychological and social factors. Experiences of bodily or emotional trauma and extreme stress, particularly in childhood, are part of the histories of many people who go on to become schizophrenic. Sustained, intensive psychotherapy can make a big difference, particularly at the onset of their illness, in whether patients will recover or at least improve their condition over time. Psychoanalytically informed treatment approaches are especially important in this regard, as they are focused not so much on teaching the patient skills to cope with the cognitive and behavioral symptoms of their illness as much as on providing them with an ongoing relationship to someone with whom they might share their experience as they live through it over a significant period of time. Unfortunately, this kind of psychotherapy is not part of the usual treatment scenario for patients suffering from schizophrenia, either in the 1990s or today. Furthermore, psychotherapists working solely in private practice outside the public sector will rarely have the opportunity to treat such patients unless they also have a support team of medical and social services personnel with whom they can coordinate the patients' care. The sad reality is that many of the homeless mentally ill people that we see today are those who have dropped out of any form of treatment program or have been deprived, as a matter of public policy, of just the kind of asylum Wingfield had formerly provided.

Schizophrenics remain the least well understood, most avoided, stigmatized, and neglected of all seriously disabled people. One in five will be homeless in any given year and approximately one in ten will commit suicide. Many will manage to lead relatively independent lives with the aid of medication, family, and community support, but a relapse into acute psychosis at some point is more likely than not. One way or another, their lives will have been utterly derailed by the illness, of which they will never be entirely cured. At an estimated incidence of one in every hundred people, or approximately 3.2 million in the United States, they are indeed the most visible invisibles in our midst.

This book has been more than twenty-five years in the making. It is derived from the nearly illegible notes I scribbled down in a small pocket notebook that I always carried with me during my internship. I typed them up originally as "process notes" to present to my supervisor at the time, an eccentric, paradoxical, and enigmatic psychoanalyst who had been a protegé of Theodor Reik, who himself was a protegé of Freud, and the author of a famous book titled *Listening with the Third Ear*. This kind of "psychoanalytic listening," with its recognition of the unconscious processes governing and informing the interactions between analyst and patient, was the foundation of my training.

In retrospect, I think there were two fundamental principles that guided me into this experience, both of which go against the view that schizophrenia is a progressively debilitating and incurable brain disease. The first is that the patient's symptoms have meaning, that what they say and do can be understood as expressive of all-too-human fears and wishes, agonies and longings, and are not simply meaningless noise, the "word salad" produced by a burnt-out, neurologically disordered brain. Second, that no matter how deeply the patient has withdrawn into a seemingly impenetrable bubble of solitude, or how much they seem to be living in a private world of hallucinations and delusions, there remains at their core a thinking, feeling, human person who might still be brought into meaningful relationship with the therapist, given enough time, patience, and willingness on both sides. According to these principles, schizophrenia is not a diagnosis of hopelessness, unless all those who might care for the patient have themselves become hopeless.

Even though the patients at Wingfield constituted a virtual textbook of psychopathology, my purpose in being there was very different from learning how to recognize and identify the various symptoms of their illness and make diagnostic assessments. I recall a conversation I had with the chief administrator of Haddon House, Dr. Walter Peterson, just a couple of weeks after I had begun my tenure on the ward. Dr. Peterson was a warm, friendly man who had been at Wingfield for many years.

"You seem to be getting the hang of being around the ladies pretty well," he said.

"Thank you, Dr. Peterson. So far, so good, I think."

"But from what I've gathered, you've not done any serious graduate work in clinical psychology. Can you distinguish between flight of ideas and loose association? Can you tell an organic brain syndrome from a severe depression? Have you ever given an intelligence test? Come with me. I want to show you something."

He wanted me to see a patient he conceived of as a paradigm example of "loosening of associations," one of the so-called "thought disorders" used to diagnose schizophrenia. We went to the women's ward and he sought her out, then took her into a small room off the corridor and got her talking. She seemed very frightened and vulnerable. Her associations did not seem all that "loose" to me, although she did make reference to volcanoes, hurricanes, and other natural disasters, which were normalized, I thought, by her explaining that these were pictures she cut out from magazines and kept in a folder by her bed. It also occurred to me that these images were a figurative way for her to represent what she was feeling, or what, in some way or other, had happened to her in her life.

Back in his office, Dr. Peterson leaned back in the chair behind his desk, which was piled high with all the files and papers having to do with his administrative work.

"Sometimes I feel like I'm in an insane asylum," he chuckled.

"That's a good one," I replied.

He asked me what I was hoping to learn here. I told him that I was here to observe patients—watch what they do, listen to what they say, and to keep track of my feelings while I was interacting with them. I said that this could help me to understand them and had everything to do with the particular kind of psychotherapy I was learning how to do. He found this all very interesting, like a revelation.

"It's experiential," he said. "You're here to study yourself."

"That's true," I said, "but in studying myself, I'm also studying them."

He asked me what this place was for me. I thought about this for a moment and told him it was like a gray box with a lot a strange jewels in it. Each one was unique and infinitely complex. I'd never seen anything like them before.

"I'm here to learn how to just *be* with these patients in a way that might have some therapeutic value," I said. "And they're the ones who can best teach me that."

Aside from the fact that each of the women on the ward seemed to be living in her own private world, it was hard for me to comprehend how they could all be suffering from the same disease. No two were alike. Understanding any one of them seemed more suited to the skills of an anthropologist. What struck me most forcefully in my first encounters with these women was the extent to which they had lost any sense of connection or continuity with the world from which they had come. Not one could tell the story of her life in any coherent way, and many had replaced whatever identity they may have once had with a mythological or supernatural account of who, what, and where they were.

Here's an example: I was outside the building in the fenced-in courtyard where some of the patients went for smoking breaks. Some kind of an altercation was going on in the wooden gazebo. Marianne, a woman I had never seen before, was arguing with a therapy aide. This was her second day on the ward after having been transferred here from the so-called "secure unit," where the more acutely disturbed, potentially violent patients were housed. Marianne insisted on smoking two cigarettes at once and the therapy aide didn't want to let her. I introduced myself to her and she took immediate notice of me. I told her that she'd have more tobacco to smoke if she finished the first one before she started the second. She seemed to agree and stubbed out the first one after she had smoked it down to the filter. The therapy aide gave her a light to start up the second, and Marianne began talking.

"I'm a keeper of shrines. I was killed at an early age and brought back to life by Aquaman after three or three thousand years."

"You're here," I said.

She told me she had the power to travel through space and mentioned several companions who went on these voyages with her. I asked her if she'd take me sometime. She considered this and said she would. I thanked her for talking and left her to smoke the rest of her second cigarette. Later that day, back upstairs in the ward, Marianne was sitting quietly alone by the windows. The nurse came to her, bringing an envelope with her name on it. It contained things that had been left behind when Marianne was transferred here. In the envelope were three baby photos. She looked at them, put them down on the chair, got up and went to the other side of the room. I went over carrying the pictures.

"Are these yours?"

"No."

She looked at them.

"I don't even know who they are," she said.

I left the pictures with her and went off.

The sense of radical dislocation, of having irretrievably lost the world from which one came, was not foreign to my own experience. Both of my parents had come to the States in flight from the Nazi occupation of Belgium in May 1940. My mother was nineteen and my father twenty-three when they finally settled, along with their parents, brothers, and sisters, in New York in 1941. Though they never shared much of their experience with my brother and me, among themselves they continued to speak several European languages for the rest of their lives. They remained closely connected to several other Jewish families who had all been in the diamond business in Antwerp before the war and had managed to get out before it was too late. I was born in New York in 1946, the first child of the whole extended family to be born on American soil. I always felt that the whole world they had left behind didn't exist anymore, that it would never be there for me, and that I had been delivered into a new world my family didn't really know or understand.

Although I could indirectly experience this feeling of losing something forever, it cannot compare to the utter eradication of self-identity found in chronic, ingrained psychosis. Not only could these women never go home again, they had become strangers to the former self that had been exiled in the first place. Many expressed the conviction that they had already died, been reborn in a new form, or continued to exist as a corpse that never got buried. Being in the presence of such a profoundly alienated person can be deeply disturbing and may account for the commonly held belief that, by the time a patient arrives at this stage of chronic illness, no form of talk therapy is practical or even possible. The memory of one's personal history, the ability to know and reflect on one's thoughts and feelings—none of this can be assumed to have survived the psychic devastation of chronic schizophrenia.

The psychoanalytic view of this condition is that the violent destruction of meaning, the relentless retreat from interpersonal relatedness, the wholesale inability to endure living in the here and now, is ultimately defensive in nature, a radical way of ridding the mind of an overwhelming mental anguish and terror that threatens to annihilate it. In the deepest states of schizophrenic withdrawal, the person is ultimately seeking to become mindless altogether. And in becoming mindless, they also become objectless, unable to share their mental space with anyone. It is crucial to understand that this is not a voluntary, willful, or even conscious decision. They had not chosen to be in this condition and could not simply "snap out of it." If they could, they wouldn't be in the hospital in the first place.

By the time I got to the hospital, I had learned enough not to assume that any of these patients would be capable of admitting, or willing to admit, a fully human presence into their field of awareness. I was prepared to be consigned to the nonhuman environment, assuming the role of an inert object. Nothing could be interpreted, confronted, or challenged. On the contrary, the delusions, hallucinations, visions, and other bizarre construals of "reality," as well as the need for emotional distance, had to be respected and understood as vital to each patient's psychic survival, as impaired as it had already become.

If I had any theoretical approach directing my encounters with the patients described in this book, it was basically this: I was simply hoping to be admitted into their *presence.* I was aiming to convey from the start the feeling that I meant them no harm, that I would make no demands or do anything that could be experienced as invasive or threatening. It was never my intention to implement any kind of pre-conceived treatment to "cure" them of their madness. My whole effort was to *make contact* with them on any terms they could tolerate and to create a setting of safety and trust, with the hope that each of them, in her own unique way, would then teach me how to listen to her, respond to her, and be with her. Thus, I hoped to become a matrix, or container, for any transformative psychic change she was willing and able to find possible. I was not, in other words, aiming to do something *to* her, but rather to gradually become something *for* her.

I began my tenure on the ward in June 1994. My father had passed away seven years earlier, and I was spending one day a week with my mother in New York, where she worked at the foreign language desk for visitors to the Metropolitan Museum of Art. We had always been very closely attached, but since my father's passing, I had become even more involved in looking after her. She was a glamorous woman with a fun-loving, playful personality, but with a hysterical streak running not far below the surface. Though seventy-two at the time, nothing about her seemed old, and I was not aware of any physical ailments that were concerning her. In October 1995, my second year on the ward, she undertook some tests on the recommendation of her doctor, which revealed a suspicious lesion in her ovary. She went into Mount Sinai Hospital toward the end of December for what was to be an exploratory surgery and developed a heart arrhythmia before the procedure could be performed. She died of congestive heart failure on December 30, my forty-ninth birthday.

Schizophrenia is the realm of the ineffable, the unthinkable, the unspeakable. My mother's dying was, at that time, unthinkable to me. It was, however, not her doctor, and certainly not she herself who gave me an inkling of what might come to pass, but rather Lucia, who, several weeks earlier, had, out of the blue, asked me, "How much for the funeral?" This was not the first time that Lucia had seemed to know things about my past and future that defied rational explanation.

It is clear to me now, in retrospect, that living through the shock of losing my mother so suddenly amplified the degree of empathic identification I could feel with those whose whole world had been shattered, the binding of their psychic firmament undone in one irrevocable stroke. Returning to the hospital soon after the funeral, I felt for the first time that the ward could be *my* asylum, *my* sanctuary, and that Lucia, in particular, intuitively sensed what had happened, offering long stretches of silent communion, which I gratefully accepted.

Our sanity is a fragile thing, built to a large extent on the ongoing continuity of the lifeworld in which we have come to know who and what we are, where we belong, and with whom we share our lives. Things happen that we may experience as catastrophic shocks, or ruptures, or irreparable losses, and that is when we may feel that we are losing our minds. Whether we succumb to psychosis at such a juncture is not predictable by any means. Nevertheless, I think it does remind us that the forces that hold our minds together, particularly at times of stress or trauma, or when we find ourselves at the threshold of the unknown, are the same as those that fell apart for each of the women described in this book. These forces comprise the structure of our subjectivity—what makes us recognizable and knowable to ourselves and makes the world intelligible to us. If that structure breaks down, we lose our sense of who and what we are, as well as any secure contact with whatever "reality" has come to define our being in the world. We can become lost in time and space. There is undoubtedly a neurological counterpart to these radical alterations of perception and cognition that go along with having a psychotic break, but we don't know very much about that yet. Lucia put this very well when she said, "I suffer all the little children to come unto me. Babies suffer. I know everything. When the baby can't go on anymore, a switch goes off . . . do you understand? Nerves and cells take over."

I wrote this book to convey my experience of engaging with three women whose minds had been consumed by schizophrenia, but also to portray them as unique human beings whose lives intersected with mine at a particular time and place and who remain forever alive in me. My intent is to recreate the experience as it happened, rather than interpret or explain it. To that end, I portray these interactions in the form of scenes, vignettes, and dialogue. The women each spoke in a uniquely original poetry of her own invention, which I had to learn to hear. Each of them can be understood in her own way as poignantly human, much more like ourselves than not—as challenging as this may be for us to accept.

The book is composed in three parts, which recount, in sequence, the unfolding of my relationships with the women I call Agnes, Mrs. Lutzky, and Lucia. With each of them, I have sought to depict an evolving process of engagement that progressed well beyond my initial hope of simply "making contact" and "being admitted into their presence."

Agnes, the most childlike of the three, was also the most fragmented in her thought process and most prone to inflicting harm on herself. She was also the patient who most adamantly insisted that she had already died. She told me that she stepped in front of an oncoming train: "It's good for you. It's not bad for you. I wasn't killed. I came back to life and was resurrected." On other occasions, she told me that she bled to death in the shower, that her parents flushed her down the toilet, that she jumped in a snake pit, and that she killed herself. On the other hand, she has said, "I'm not suicidal . . . Something happened. Something happened. Something happened. God . . . God . . . God . . . God . . . I woke up brand new." Over the time we were together, she progressed from being unwilling to ever leave the ward for fear of falling down the stairs or throwing herself to her death, to being given permission to leave the ward unattended to feed the birds and clean their cages on another floor of the building. We played and sang together. Finally, she was able to go down the stairs with me, one step at a time—this from a woman who, although she could not consciously remember or even comprehend it now, had fallen down a flight of stairs in a baby carriage as a toddler, an accident that killed her mother.

Mrs. Lutzky brought out the playful side of my personality in a way that enabled me to transform her relentless onslaught of paranoid delusions of torture, mutilation, and persecution into something like a Jewish comedy routine. Although I could make her laugh and smile with my teasing and comically sadistic jokes, I never saw her shed a tear, or express any form of tenderness toward anyone on the ward. She was the only one of the three women described here who exhibited catatonic withdrawal from all interpersonal engagement whatsoever: she would sometimes get up from her chair, stand motionless before the windows, and silently stare out into space for long stretches. She began by accusing me of killing her mother and telling me that I would die like an animal. She persisted in calling me "Dr. Mengele," after the Nazi physician who performed deadly medical experiments on prisoners in the concentration camps, but was soon telling me to go out and buy all kinds of fancy jewelry for both of us since she was the richest woman in the world. She gave me recipes and ordered enormous quantities of Chinese food and Jewish delicatessen out of the air. She ended up wishing we could be married—no sex, but a lot of shopping and driving around. Her paranoid delusions never diminished over the whole time we were together, and I think now, in retrospect, that my comedic playfulness was a way of defending myself from what I sometimes experienced as an exhausting verbal and

emotional assault. I felt that a part of her knew, albeit deeply re-
pressed, that the elaborate delusional world she inhabited was a brittle
and desperate defense against even more devastating feelings of aban-
donment, bitterness, and despair. I was not about to try to take that
away from her, as there was nothing to put in its place.

My relationship with Lucia was the most emotionally complex of
them all. At various times, she experienced me and spoke to me as
though I were her baby boy, her father, her husband, the father of her
imaginary children, and her doctor. I, in turn, had reciprocal feelings
toward her. I experienced her sometimes as my mother, my wife, my
patient, my colleague, and my analyst. She seemed to know things
about my family history that made me feel she was clairvoyant. The
overall trajectory of our relationship was akin to a love story, and indeed she wrote several love letters to me over the course of time. The
growth of these feelings was mutual, and she was the only one of the
patients on the ward who couldn't bring herself to say goodbye when
I finally left; neither could I find a way of saying goodbye to her.

I have no way of knowing how much further I could have gone with
any of these patients had there been unlimited opportunity to continue. I had the sense that any enduring improvement would have
taken years to accomplish, if ever, and that neither they nor I could
have done it alone. These were some of the most tragic lives I have
ever encountered. My feeling upon leaving the ward was grief that I
could not have done more to help them than I did, my feelings inex-
tricably bound up with losing my mother as well. Above all, I would
like others to listen to these women, feel their presence, and begin to
grasp the magnitude of their estrangement, the depth of their loneli-
ness, and the healing power of feeling heard, understood, and perhaps
even loved.

PART I
Agnes

1

The first day.

Dr. Peterson, the clinical psychologist who has been assigned to look after me, tells me to watch two patients, Agnes and Hilary. A nurse is giving a class called Mental and Physical Health. The entire group of about fifteen women is talking at once. Agnes, though appearing middle aged, has the voice and nonstop insistence on calling attention to herself of a nursery school child. The high-pitched, infantile voice is uncanny, coming from this face and this body. She's in constant motion, raising her hand to be called on and interrupting. Hilary says nothing, but when called upon gives extremely concise and assured answers.

Nurse: "What's the opposite of healthy?"

Hilary: "Dirty is the opposite of healthy. Healthy is when you're cooked."

Nurse: "Why would the doctor take you into the examination room?"

Agnes: "Because he loves you and he wants to save your life."

Agnes says later that God wants her blessed.

There follows a discussion of whether it's normal to feel like killing yourself.

Hilary: "It's not exceptional."

Hilary has, in fact, been found hoarding pills in her room. She has recently been moved here after eight years in another building where she was kept in a more secure environment. Dr. Peterson tells me that in the past she has bitten him through his jacket and has also collected and eaten feces.

Same class the following week.

The topic for discussion is "Mind and Body." The nurse is telling the patients that they have both a mind and a body.

Hilary: "I'm a mind without a body."

Agnes is nowhere to be seen but her shrill, childlike voice penetrates the room from the adjoining bathroom, where she is asking and answering questions though the wall. The nurse tells her to get back into the classroom. She walks straight toward me, stops, and announces, "Dr. Poser, I've got popcorn in my rectum."

2

Agnes is absent from the regular morning health class. The nurse tells me that she had to be kept upstairs because she had "deteriorated" over the weekend and had to be put in "five point restraint" (wrists, waist, and ankles) following an episode of running amok, naked, thrashing and flailing about on the ward. The nurse asks if I would like to see her. I say that I would. I find Agnes on the ward corridor dressed in a sheet and surrounded by two attendants. I ask her whether she would like to talk with me. She says she would. The nurse gives her a paper cup filled with milk. We go to a corner of the dayroom and sit down on a couch, leaving one seat empty between us. One of the therapy aides sits on a chair near Agnes's end of the couch.

She looks like a broken doll. Her infantile voice is charged with urgency, panic, and terror. She says she filled the entire bathroom with menstrual blood and that there was a cord around her neck from a Cabbage Patch doll that would have taken her head off if she hadn't managed to remove it herself in the toilet. She shows me her neck where the wound was. There is no wound. She tells me she's terribly frightened of dolls. She shows me other nonexistent wounds—one in her hand from running a sewing needle through her finger, the other on her feet, which she says are deformed baby feet and that she has to wear braces and special Buster Brown shoes in order to walk and that she had been bitten by a shark when she was a baby swimming in the ocean but her mother didn't recognize it or didn't believe it when she told her.

She tells me she is telling the truth.

I tell her I believe her.

She takes a few sips of milk and gradually becomes less agitated. I ask her if she would like to continue seeing me on a regular basis. She says she would.

She repeats that she is telling the truth.

I repeat that I believe her.

Forty-five minutes have transpired. She sits calmly sipping her milk. I tell her that we have to stop now but that I will see her next week. I thank her for talking and get up to leave.

On the way out, I see the nurse. She says there are a few things I should know about Agnes. She is diagnosed as "schizophrenic, disorganized type." Her biography includes the information that at the age of two she fell down a flight of stairs in a baby carriage, and in the accident her mother was killed. I immediately have a vivid recollection of the famous scene in the Russian filmmaker Sergei Eisenstein's *Battleship Potemkin* in which a mother is ruthlessly gunned down by Cossacks at the top of the Odessa Steps and her baby in the baby carriage goes careening down the steps all the way to the bottom. I can't follow anything after that and leave the building.

3

The night before my next visit to the hospital, I have a dream of Agnes: Asleep in my bed, I hear her unmistakable voice and realize that she's in the house. The voice continues nonstop in Agnes's usual way. I hear her coming up the stairs, along the hall, and then into my bedroom. She climbs into bed with me like a child and curls up in a fetal position with her back to me on my left.

Health class the following day.

The nurse isn't there. I'm asked to begin leading the class. I tell the group that the nurse isn't here yet and ask whether it would be all right if I start off the class with them. They seem to like this idea. I tell them that we can do anything they would like to do and ask for suggestions. Mrs. Lutzky asks whether we could invent something. I ask her what she would like to invent. She says, "A car that you couldn't get hurt in." I say, "So, you would like to feel safe. That's a very good thing to talk about." She agrees. The class gets enthusiastic about this. The nurse comes in and I tell her what we're doing. She thinks this is a good topic. She goes around the room asking for synonyms for "safe." She asks whether feeling safe is a good feeling or a bad feeling.

Hilary: "I prefer a dangerous feeling to a safe feeling."

The nurse presents the example of standing in front of an oncoming train.

Agnes: "I did that! I stepped in front of a train! It's good for you! It's not bad for you! I wasn't killed! I came back to life and was resurrected!"

The nurse introduces the topic of safe sex. She asks the patients whether they know what a condom is and what you do with it.

Nicole: "You put a condom on your head to protect your brain."

Agnes: "I don't believe in sex any more."

Nicole: "I think you put it on your head and leave it."

Agnes goes to the bathroom. She's flushing the toilet over and over, maybe a dozen times. The nurse goes in after her.

Nurse: "Agnes, why are you flushing paper towels down the toilet? Don't you know that we've had stopped-up toilets on the ward every day?"

In fact, the patients have been flushing panties and other items down the toilets on the ward.

Agnes: "It's water; it cleanses you! I'm putting paper towels down the toilet because I want to put out the fire!"

She repeats several times over the next twenty minutes, "Why don't we put out the fire?"

There follows a discussion of teeth and learning how to swallow.

Agnes: "I swallowed a lead pipe because I have a mental problem! My IQ is too high! I need a bodyguard!"

Ms. G, a very large woman in the back of the room, is stuffing her shirt into her mouth. Agnes is tightening the cord of her hooded sweatshirt around her neck.

The class is over. Agnes thanks me for taking care of her on the ward this morning. I was never there.

4

Agnes comes and takes the vacant seat next to me. Another patient, Katie, is nearby, strapped into a "geriatric chair" and rocking the entire apparatus so violently I'm afraid it's going to tip over on the floor.

"Shut up!" she's screaming. "Shut the fuck up, you fat pig!"

There's no one talking to her.

"What's wrong with her?" I ask Agnes.

"Her mouth is all steel. There's a reason for everything. You've got to investigate. I'm six years old. My brains won't set me free. But I'm doing better. It's all part of slowing down my process. I'm calm."

"You seem calm."

Then she stands up with her body directly in front of me.

"This is me," she says (looking at herself), "is that you?" (looking at me).

"Yes," I say, "this is me."

5

Coming onto the ward, I can hear Agnes screaming, bawling, and sobbing even before I enter the dayroom, where I see her sprawled across two chairs by the window. I go over and sit down.

"Dr. Poser, I'm going to take you to court!" she screams at me. "You don't dress me properly! Look at me! I'm in baby clothes! These are my pajamas! Go jump in a snake pit like I did! Go kill yourself like I did! Because you don't give a fuck! I take a shower and I'm beautiful! They put the raggiest, shittiest clothes in the world on me! I didn't eat breakfast! If it continues, I'm not going to eat lunch! I'm not going to eat dinner! I can't smile! You put the raggiest, shittiest clothes on me! I cut my arm! It won't come off! Why won't it come off? Because you're a bitch, that's why!"

She goes back to crying and bawling.

The nurse comes over and asks whether she would like to go to her room and lie down for a while. She resists. The nurse says she would like Agnes to go to her bed. She helps her to get up and walks her out of the dayroom, Agnes unleashing a stream of incomprehensible accusations at me at the top of her lungs all the way down the corridor.

A patient walks through dayroom singing: "*Praise the Lord above / The Father has spoken to us / Speak the holy name . . .*"

Another patient mumbling in the corner fills the entire dayroom with a sound like a motor running in neutral.

6

I stop by the nursing station on my way to the dayroom and see the ward psychiatrist sitting at his desk. I take the opportunity to ask him about Agnes. He says that this most recent episode is part of a history of her going into a dissociated state in which, totally oblivious of what she's doing, she has seriously wounded or bruised herself and needs to be sedated and restrained until she regains her composure. The problem is compounded by the fact that she has vivid hallucinations of these injuries and can become extremely agitated while in their grip. He said he was trying to adjust her medications but there was not much more he could do to prevent her from inflicting any more harm on herself. While I'm sitting there, Agnes staggers in, weeping and bawling like a baby.

"My pants are full of blood!" she cries, sees me, and turns toward me with both arms outstretched.

"Help me! Help me!"

I don't know what to do. I am appalled and shaken. The nurse takes her into the seclusion room.

7

I hear Agnes wailing as soon as I come into the ward. I have been advised to stay away from her when she is "like this," to be cordial but not to try to engage her in any extended conversation that might prove too stimulating for her. Entering the dayroom, I see she is stretched across two chairs, screaming, crying, and moaning. She's on her back with one leg and one arm up in the air, making trembling, delicate movements with the thumb and forefinger of her upraised hand.

I sit down next to Mrs. Lutzky so I can see Agnes, but make no attempt to contact her. Mrs. Lutzky tells me that she gave birth to a beautiful turkey bird and that she did all kinds of things to take care of it. It comes to her window at night and gets into bed with her.

Agnes gets up and goes into the bathroom. She's wailing and moaning from inside one of the toilet stalls. She stays in there a very long time. I can't understand anything she's saying.

She comes back into the dayroom. She's screaming, crying, and wailing, curled up in a chair with her knees tucked up to her chest. Dr. Peterson comes in. I ask him whether I can talk to Agnes for a few minutes. I want to calm her down. I go over and ask her if she would like to talk with me. She leans toward me as though wanting to fall into my arms. I back off and tell her that I can't talk to her if she continues screaming and ask her if she would be capable of stopping. She nods like a wide-eyed child and stops. I pull over another chair and put it under her feet so she's not curled up in a ball. Every time she starts to talk, she cries. I'm not following her very well. She's afraid she's going to be attacked in some way. I tell her she will not be attacked by anyone here. She's both terrified and angry. She says she has no mother or father to take care of her, that they left her to die, that they flushed her down the toilet. I'm feeling her psychic pain come in surges of utter terror and complete helplessness. I keep thinking of what the psychoanalyst Donald Winnicott describes as the unspeakable agony of trauma endured in infancy, that what happened to her cannot be remembered now because there was then no coherent mind capable of experiencing it. All that remains, Winnicott says, is the primal terror of falling down the stairs, endlessly and forever.

She's quiet. I stay with her silently for a while. I ask her whether she feels calm. She says she does. I go back to Dr. Peterson. He tells me to go outside the building and take a break. From the parking lot I hear her screaming all the way down from the fourth floor.

8

I go into a quiet corner of the dayroom in order to give Agnes a chance to talk to me in relative privacy. She's been waiting. She comes and stretches out on two chairs with me seated next to her and writing. She's composed, relatively calm, pensive. Her speech becomes fragmentary: "Blood . . . shower, shower . . . She wouldn't feed me . . . I had third degree burns . . . I bled to death in the shower and I can't stay here any more . . . I had a fish hook . . . whether it was done deliberately or an accident I don't know . . ."

Now she's crouching on the footstool in front of her chair, as though recovering from an assault. She wants new shoes. I ask her what kind of shoes she wants. She brightens and seems happy to be thinking about this.

"Brown shoes, moccasins . . . Buster Brown moccasins. I'd like to get out of here but I'm afraid. I'm afraid I might jump to my death. My hand went flying into his eye. I didn't do it on purpose."

She says she has to go the bathroom; would I excuse her?

"Of course."

She goes. She comes back. She admires my watch. A green watch. I tell her I got it on Canal Street. She says that she used to get lost on Canal Street, that she also used to get lost on the subway.

"I'd call my mother to find out how to get home."

"So, you can get lost and still find your way home."

"Yes, I used to make dinner. I'd make lasagna in the oven."

She says she has to go to the bathroom again. I excuse her.

She comes back and resumes talking.

"They don't understand. I'm educated. I'm intelligent. They just don't understand."

"Do you want me to understand?"

"Yes."

"How can I help you?"

"I don't know."

"Would it help you for me to understand you?"

"Yes."

She pauses.

"My mother sent me out."

"What for?"

"To grow up."

We're quiet for a while.

"It's enough for today," she says.

I sit with her a few more moments in silence before I get up and leave the dayroom.

I go outside and see a man playing with a dog. The man throws a stick and the dog brings it back. It's a black and brown German shepherd. I join them. The man is the medical doctor for the building. The dog's name is Barney. The doctor tells me that he brought the dog to the hospital as a puppy and raised him on the wards, so all the patients know him. I play fetch with Barney. The doctor likes it here. He says it's a more regular day than working on an emergency unit where you might see thirty or forty patients in a day. I ask him about Agnes's condition. He says that every time she's hurt herself they've had a look at her in the clinic and so far they've been able to patch her up without needing to operate. Beyond that, there's not much else they can do. He says there are some very sick people here. He goes off for a walk with Barney on the hospital grounds. It's a beautiful day.

9

The week after Thanksgiving.

Coming into the ward, I am greeted immediately by Agnes, who asks if today is Thursday. I tell her it is. I ask her whether they gave her nice things to eat for Thanksgiving. She says that she "ate and ate 'til I made myself better." She says something about taking a shower.

Teresa, a tiny, hyper-energetic woman with black pigtails who calls me "Father," interrupts us to ask me for the body of Christ.

Agnes goes off to the windows and opens one, saying that she's letting in a breeze. She comes back.

"I'm grown up now. I had a bagel and coffee for breakfast. It agrees with me. . . . You're taking good care of me. I have polio again. You're taking good care of me."

"You're taking good care of me."

"No, it's the other way around. They saved my life. They didn't want me to die. I woke up brand new. I don't want to hurt anybody. I don't want to choke on my food. I'm drinking milk. I don't want to fall apart. I don't want my body to break, my heart, my bones. I had open-heart surgery. Nobody came to visit. Excuse me for drinking in front of you."

I excuse her.

"We're not in the community. We're in a mental institution. They're protecting me. I get escorted to the vending machines so I don't get raped in the elevator. I think we should put out the fire."

She starts rocking back and forth. "It's me, it's me, it's me . . ."
She goes away. She comes back.

"Did you miss me?" she asks.

"Did you miss me?"

"Yes. I didn't want to leave you alone," she replies.

"Then I shouldn't leave you alone."

"Right! God loves me with his whole heart and soul."

She goes away.

Now she's across the room with another patient. This woman is singing the "Hokey Pokey" song: "*You put your right foot in / You take your right foot out / You put your right foot in / And you shake it all about / You do the hokey pokey / And you turn yourself around / That's what it's all about . . .*" She repeats the same verse for the left foot, right hand, left hand, et cetera . . . Agnes is entranced. She joins in the singing, then starts dancing. I go over to join them.

"Dr. Poser . . . Agnes!" she exclaims.

She's laughing, delighted, utterly childlike. She continues singing and dancing and wants me to dance, too. I do a few steps, laugh with her, and leave the dayroom.

10

Agnes comes and sits down beside me. She says she wants to go back to work but also wants to be taken care of. I tell her about my going to the dentist. She tells me that if I get sick in the dentist's office, I should take holy water. She says that she died in the dentist's chair, had Holy Communion, and had holy water put on her eye. That it opened the eye. She tells me I have to be wise. I say that she has to teach me how to be wise. She says the doctor opened her eyes to the world.

"I don't want you to die on me," she says.

"I don't want *you* to die on *me*," I reply.

She startles at this and looks at me very intensely in the eyes. Then she relaxes back into her chair.

"I haven't been out in ages. I'm not greedy. I left home and came here because I knew I wasn't getting loved. Twenty-six years. I'm not ready."

"How can I help you?"

"Just talk to me."

Mrs. Lutzky seems to have lost something and says from across the room that Agnes flushed it down the toilet. Agnes overhears this and says she did not. Then, to me, she says, "She's dreaming. I'm making myself somebody in the world. This is me."

I tell her about the Christmas vacation coming up and how I will be away for two weeks.

"You're going to miss me," she says.

"Yes, I will miss you," I reply.

She talks about mopping floors, cleaning the bathroom. I ask her if she knows the story of Cinderella, that she's just like Cinderella. She becomes extremely happy, laughing, full of delight. She knows about the glass slipper and that dreams come true in fairy tales.

"Rapunzel, Rapunzel, let down your hair. This is a castle. This is a mental institution," she says.

She excuses herself to "go peepee."

She comes back with a small container of milk.

"I got my milk. It's a life saver."

She starts drinking hungrily out of the container.

"Excuse me. I'm drinking. I don't want to be rude. I was going to get sick and die so I came here."

She goes off to throw away the empty container.

She comes back. We're looking at the Christmas decorations they have put up around the dayroom—plastic Santa Clauses and a tree with plastic decorations. I start humming and then singing "Deck the Halls." When I get to "*Fa la la la la . . .*" she joins in, then bursts into laughter and what seems like utter bliss. We sing another chorus.

"I let out gas sometimes," she says, apologetically. "I have to have my diapers changed. It's my liver, my gall bladder."

An aide comes in with a rolling table filled with snacks, pretzels and cheese crackers. This is a treat for the patients. Agnes is up immediately and returns with a bag of Cheese Nibs. She doesn't open it with her fingers but puts the packet directly into her mouth and tears it open with her teeth in one ripping bite. I am struck by the primal force of this. She then lays the contents out neatly on her lap and proceeds to consume them all in a few moments.

There are leftover snacks on the rolling table. The aide offers me one. I first decline, then ask Agnes if she would like another. She says she would. I go up and take a Cheese Nibs packet and give it to her. She repeats her earlier performance almost exactly. When she's done, she asks me to wish her a Merry Christmas. I wish her a Merry Christmas. We quietly sing another round of "Deck the Halls."

"I love a clean body," she says. "I'm for real. I'm here. I'm in reality. I'm here. I'm the best patient they've got. I just sit in the dayroom." She excuses herself to go to the bathroom. "I want to make sure I'm clean." She comes back. She expresses concern for me, that I might get sick by being around the dayroom so long. I tell her I appreciate her concern, that I'm feeling fine.

"I handle myself gracefully," she says.

I ask her if she'd like to go to the window. She comes. We look out together.

"What do you see?"

She points out various parts of the building, air conditioning vents, and so on, nothing of the landscape and houses beyond.

"I need a chaperone. I don't want to get raped in the elevator. I'm afraid to leave."

We sit down for a while in silence and I tell her it's time for me to go now. She doesn't look up when I leave.

11

We're looking at a voluptuous red blossom about to burst open on a thick green stalk.

"What's that?" I ask her.

"It's an amaryllis."

"Ever have a flower garden?"

"We had grapevines in a little garden behind the house. My father made wine for the family. I'd take care of them."

"Could you still do it now?"

"It was a long time ago."

She goes to the bathroom and flushes the toilet. She goes over to another patient on the other side of the dayroom, talks with her for a minute or two, and comes back with half a sandwich, which she consumes in one mouthful before she returns to her seat next to me.

"I'm frustrated! The dentist! My mouth! I eat too fast!"

"Do you know why?"

"Reverse combat! I've come back! It's taking a long time! I hurt my feet! If I don't eat, I'm going to die!"

"Eat."

"Me, I'm making it! If I hadn't eaten, I would have died at the breakfast table! You saved my life! If I don't sit here drinking milk, I would have died! It's over! The needle!"

She pauses to observe another patient sitting nearby.

"She's in for a lot of disappointment, that woman. The dentist," she says, pointing to her mouth, "reality came in!"

She gets up and goes to the window.

"Look, garden furniture!"

She's pointing to some white chairs on the patio of a house some distance beyond the building.

"I'm back! I'm back! Do you care?"

"Yes, I do care."

Mrs. Lutzky addresses me from her chair: "You ruined a beautiful brain, Dr. Mengele, you ruined a beautiful brain!"

Agnes continues.

"I'm not afraid of Dr. Kurtz's dog Barney. Barney won't attack me because I fed Lester."

I tell her animals are like that—they know when you have good feelings toward them.

"My dog couldn't walk well, he had small paws. I'm so glad it passed over, aren't you? It's over . . . the injections . . . dentist's needles . . . eating too fast . . ." She begins yelling. "It's over! It's over! It's over! It's over! It passed! It's over!"

She starts perspiring. "Look! Sweat's pouring out all over my face!"

"Well, why don't we just wipe it off?"

Mrs. Lutzky tells me she was a hip surgeon and a brain surgeon with Dr. Mengele. She looks at my notebook.

"How could you read that? It's a scribble!"

"I'm doing the best I can."

Agnes continues: "The boy in the apartment house . . . he's praying for me . . . I'm not married to anyone . . . otherwise I would . . . You know what I mean . . . gorilla woman . . . pocketbook . . . gorilla . . . You need to get fed to stay alive . . . just that one day . . . just that one day . . . I took a shower . . . I cleared my nose . . . a blood vessel

came out . . . I picture myself in my coffin . . . I'm breathing well . . .
My nose passage is clear . . . I can breathe very well . . ."

"You can breathe very well. You can walk, you can talk, you can
breathe. What else can you do?"

"I can have Christmas at home. The staff is proud of me . . .
somebody cares . . . and you can tell a bum when you see one, right?"

"You bet!"

"It's two thirty!" she squeals, "I made it! . . . Reality! The dentist!
It's over! It's over! It's over! It's twenty to three! It's over, Doctor, it's
over! . . . Help me talk . . . I used to be an outpatient, now I'm an in-
patient. I'm smart, Doctor, I'm smart, I'm a smartie."

"It's time for me to go now."

"I'll walk you to the door."

We walk out of the dayroom and down the corridor in silence.
When we get to the end, she says, "Good night, Doctor," and shakes
my hand. I leave the ward.

Outside the building, I see Martha, another patient from the
ward. She's on a smoking break.

"What are you hanging around here like some kind of police-
man? Go on," she shouts, "get out of here! You don't belong in this
world!"

12

Agnes is sitting by the window. I go over and tell her I brought some potting soil for the amaryllis. "That's very nice of you," she says, "I died in the dentist's chair . . . I took holy water . . . My mother and father warned me about dentists, Dr. Poser, my mother and father warned me. This is a new world . . . a new generation . . . I worked hard for this every day . . . coming here and starting a new life with women . . . I had a real job. They said okay, let's see what you can do. Let's see how you perform. I jumped down the basement steps head first! I died in the dentist's chair and came back! I stepped in front of a train! It was a dream come true . . . I can handle it . . . I'm forty-seven . . . I can handle it . . . These people here are bums—kissing and feeling each other up in the elevator! They're making a fool out of me! They're trying to make a fool out of me and I'm not a fool! I don't know what they want from me."

"What do you think they want?"

"My body! The whole picture's right here . . . they're witches and vampires . . . my bewitching mother brought poison to my house . . . I came here because I can't stay home with a man . . . Because I'm not a tramp! . . . Tramp! Lesbian! Whore! That's what they call me here! What do they know? I keep telling them I don't know what they're talking about . . . it makes me very angry. I came here to get away from the men! And then the audacity! Not even saying 'Good morning, how are you?' Just like a bunch of wild animals! All I know is, I have two more months to go. It's twenty to three and I know what I'm doing! They're all tramps and bums! There's something totally wrong here! I'm walking away from here!"

"You want me to help you?"

"I've got no place to go."

"What's the alternative?"

"See the picture through."

She's quiet for a moment, then, more reflectively:

"Life is history, life is destiny, and life is a pain in the ass."

"So why don't you want to get out of here?"

"I don't know what to do . . . I want my medicine . . . Reality comes here . . . It's over for me now with the dentist . . ."

I tell her I'm going to the dentist myself tomorrow.

"I wish you well. Don't run around . . . come back after you've been to the dentist . . . now you got the message . . . it's my mouth . . . they're all vampires . . . they're not women . . . they're animals . . . they want to hurt somebody."

"Do you feel like you don't belong here?"

"I do and I don't . . . reality . . . reality . . . my world was a dream world . . . a paper doll world, you know what I mean?"

"What do you mean?"

"Bicycles, ballet slippers . . ."

She tells me about her mother's making ballet costumes for her and her sister.

"How old were you then?"

"Thirteen years old . . . When you're forty-seven . . . you can't be a baby all your life in the same place . . . I got over the death part . . . I'm here. Nothing can hurt me here. You've got beachcombers, vampires, gypsies, bums . . . I just want you to know that the reason I made it is that I'm not a gypsy, I'm not a beachcomber, I'm not a bum. I went down the elevator to the vending machines one time and men were killing each other! There was blood all over the place! No more! A chaperone for me now!"

She shows me her thumb. There are small red scratches on it.

"That's from work! Factory work! A man's job! I'm not a gypsy, tramp, thief! I don't go to the bathroom any more . . . urinalysis . . . menopause . . . I'm doing the right thing! I'm forty-seven. Becky is fifty-two—she shouldn't be here any more."

"Where would you like to be when you're fifty?"

"When I'm fifty? More lady!"

"Growing up?"

"Yeah, growing up. I couldn't get the words into my head . . . I can't hide in a cubbyhole, a closet . . . What I have to do is push myself to go to the program. I didn't want to go this morning, but then I was glad I went."

"What'd you do?"

"Color pictures . . . they kept mine."

"You want me to push you?"

"You're going to have to. They're at reality . . . I've got to slow down a little. I'm pushing too fast. I don't want to be bullied; I'll have a relapse."

"Am I bullying you?"

"No."

"You'll tell me if you feel I'm bullying you."

"Yes. The time is important in this case . . . See that? It's twenty after three . . . the time is going by . . . a lot can happen in that time, a lot can happen in that time, Doctor . . . the bewitching hour . . . My roommate jumps out of bed at me yelling, banging on the walls . . . I don't even know her! It doesn't bother me to sit here talking because I know what I'm doing. I'm being a patient . . . I'm not a wallflower."

"What's a wallflower?"

"You know, girls that hang out in discos and bars, running around, that kind of thing. I go to a hospital instead . . . sexual intercourse is over . . . a lot of jealousy involved . . ."

She's quiet.

I tell her it's time for me to go now and that I will see her next week.

"Good night, Doctor."

13

A nurse comes into the dayroom and says that there's a party downstairs. We're moving out of Haddon House, the secluded building that has been home to the ward for many years. All of the patients will be transferred into another, much larger building, Langley Pavilion. It will also mark the departure of several longtime staff members, including Dr. Peterson, who has been my mentor and guide from the very beginning. I go down to the party with the patients. Dr. Hartman, the chief of psychology for the whole institution, is up front, leading the patients in singing along to a tape of "Knock Three Times."

Agnes surveys this scene and says, "Things change; they don't stay the same."

Dr. Peterson is in the hallway outside the party. It's his last day at the hospital. He's saying goodbye to several staff members. It's an awkward moment. He's been here for decades and knows many of the patients intimately. There's no way to say goodbye to them. He asks me to help him load the last boxes of papers from his office into his car. We go upstairs to get the boxes and take them out. I thank him for all he has done to help me. We shake hands and he leaves.

Back upstairs after the party, I sit with Agnes.

"I play hard to get, even the dentist asked me to marry him. I turned him down. I knew I was . . . cherry pie . . . for myself . . . family problem . . . patient money . . . I get around . . . I migrate."

She laughs. "Did I tell you that my cancer went away? I have patience of gold . . . I have a lot of patience."

She's calm. She gets up and goes to the window.

"Look! A moth! I'll get him. I'll get him, Dr. Poser. I'll get him!"

The moth is caught in the narrow space between the window and the outside screen. She tries reaching it with her hand, but it falls into the crack at the bottom of the window frame. She gets a book from a nearby shelf and hits down into the crack.

"I got him! I got him! He's dead!"

"What would happen if he escaped?"

"We could catch a disease from him."

She seems very pleased with herself.

"The dentist hugged me . . . he kissed me. I want someone to believe me. The dentist . . . are you coming to Langley Pavilion with me?"

"Yes, we're all going to Langley Pavilion."

"Your home has a lot to do with you, where you come from. I'm Irish, Italian, Indian. My mother was an Indian princess . . . My mother and father . . . we had turtles, goldfish, hamsters—they believed in all that, and going to the beach, going fishing. . . . I remember falling off a bridge driving with my father . . . I beat him up, punched him . . . I put my foot on the accelerator and fell into the river . . . falling down the stairs . . . it's a habit."

"Why is that?"

She gets agitated.

"I fell out of the roller coaster with my mother . . . she saved me."

She puts her arms around herself.

"I fell in a swamp. I don't know why I didn't come out. I didn't get up."

"You don't have to know; you may never know; you're here."

"I love my mother and father. I'm here, being a good patient, because I love my mother and father."

She's quiet. I sit with her in silence.

14

We're in the new building. I go outside. Coming out the front door, somebody throws a red and black checkered lumberjack shirt that lands on my head. I try to give it back, but nobody seems to want it. I return to the ward carrying the shirt. I approach the patient who I believe originally threw it at me and ask if it belongs to her. She says it's not hers and she doesn't want it. I go over to Agnes and ask her if she wants the shirt.

"For me? A present! Oh, thank you, Doctor Poser! A birthday present for me from Doctor Poser!"

"Let's see how it fits."

She puts it on, buttoning it up all the way to the top. She likes it very much. She asks for my notebook and writes, "Dear Dr. Poser / Thank you / Love Agnes / for the Birthday present from you!" She gives me back the notebook.

"I'm still here, I'm still here," she says.

"What are we going to do about you?"

"I don't know. I don't know."

Silence.

"Bingo . . . Do you like me? I know what I'm doing. I'm still here. What are we going to do? Protection. Protection. I don't want to be a bum. Protection. Chaperone. Baby. Can't go home. My parents are older than I am. I can't go home. My parents forbid it. Birthday parties. Chaperone. Catholic. Flashback. Feedback. Doctor Poser, thank you for saying hello to me. Doctor Poser, can I be excused to go to lunch?"

"Yes."

"What are you going to do this afternoon?"

"I'm going to see Dr. Hartman at twelve thirty."

I leave. On the way down the corridor, I pass by the entrance to the cafeteria. Mrs. Lutzky and a therapy aide are waiting to be let in. I stop and chat. Mrs. Lutzky pokes me gently in the ribs. The aide asks her, "Why are you poking at him?"

"I like him," she says.

"It's okay," I say, "she likes me."

The other patients have meanwhile taken seats at the cafeteria tables inside. I see Agnes seated at a table directly facing the doorway where I'm standing. Our eyes lock into a powerful hold for a few seconds. I leave the ward for the day.

15

Agnes is wearing a gauze patch taped over her right eye. The patch is half off, on account of her peeling off the tape, and I can see that her eye and the whole right side of her face is very inflamed. I have no idea what caused this injury. We're going downstairs to be outside in the courtyard for a while. I get on the end of the line of patients. Agnes has gone ahead. When we get to the bottom, she's waiting for me. This is the first time we've ever been outside the building together.

"You made it. I almost fell down the stairs head first. My ankle gave way."

She walks into the grassy area of the courtyard and sits down on a bench in the sun with several other patients. I leave her to her socializing, something I have hardly ever seen. After a while, she comes and sits down next to me.

"It's time we started talking again," I say.

"I know," she replies.

Silence.

She's playing with her eye patch, picking her cuticles.

"I'm intelligent."

"If I didn't know that by now, what would I know?"

"Nothing."

She's rubbing her eyes and drooling.

"How are you, Doctor Poser? Are you there?"

"I'm here."

"Hang in there, . . . I'm not a gypsy."

"What are you?"

"A regular person with feelings."

"I know that, too."

"I intend to take better care of myself . . . I feel proud of my family here . . . they let me sit here . . . they're proud of me . . . they didn't lock the doors on me. I'm proud of my family . . . I didn't fall down the stairs because you're doing a good job."

"I shouldn't let you fall."

"I slipped but I didn't fall. It's because you were there. You handled yourself like a doctor. You did your job."

The medical doctor comes into the dayroom with Barney, his dog. He's looking for Agnes. He wants to have a look at her eye and apply a fresh eye patch. She goes off with the doctor and Barney.

She rejoins me after she's finished with the doctor. She's already removed the new eye patch.

"I'm going to the beauty parlor tomorrow; I'm going to have my hair washed and set. I'm so proud of you!"

She's watching a couple on the TV screen kissing and making out.

"I'm not that!" she bursts out, "mushy, smoochy!"

She's very angry, then turns to me and changes her tone entirely.

"I'm proud of you for not letting me fall down the stairs . . . he saved my life . . . I remember you. I don't forget you. My mother saved me, give you another chance." She becomes very animated. "It's the second time you saved my life for me! That's why I'm sitting here in the chair."

"What was the first time?"

"It's because of you! Life is the greatest gift you can have! Well, I'm alive! I can't believe it! She gets softer now: "You helped me a lot on the other ward . . . I'm . . . it's . . . human being."

"What does that mean?"

"Feelings . . . character . . . culture . . . the dentist. I'm a good patient . . . You're forgiven."

More excited now: "The war is over! The war is over!"

"What do we have to do now?"

"You have to love someone."

Pause.

"I'm proud of you . . . you can say, 'I have saved a woman's life in this world.'"

We get up and she walks with me down the corridor. As we get toward the end, she says, "You protect me."

"Thank you for telling me that."

16

Agnes is curled up in a chair by the window, apparently asleep. The nurse announces that it's time to go outside for a ten-minute break. She wakes up. She's waiting for me to go with her. She says she's afraid of falling down the stairs. I tell her she's not going to fall. I go first, she follows, holding on to the banister and taking one step at a time. When we get to the bottom, she thanks me and goes on into the courtyard.

Back in the dayroom, Agnes is sitting by the door and starts laughing when she sees me. She shows me the drawing she made in her class. She asks me to sit down and wishes me a happy Father's Day. I thank her.

"I'm not afraid to die."

"You're not afraid to live, are you?"

She laughs.

"I need a roof over my head."

She starts talking about her father and mother. She tells me that her father worked in a shipyard. They wanted to send him to Virginia but he didn't want to go, and became a machinist instead. She says that she didn't want to lose me. I tell her that I will be here until Christmas. She counts out the months between now and Christmas, July through December, six months.

"Would you like me to take you with me when I go?"

She laughs. She says that she wants me to come back after lunch, no more picking nails. ". . . Protection . . . the best I could do . . . can't be alone . . . need an escort . . . work . . . This is a very touching moment. Do you know that?"

"Yes, I know that."

"I'm laughing all day that you're here, I'm very lonely. I'm very lonely."

When it's time for me to leave, she walks me down the hall and I tell her I will see her next week.

"Good night, Doctor Poser."

17

Agnes is sitting in a chair handling four dollar bills. She tells me she got paid and that she won the plastic medallion she is wearing around her neck playing Bingo. She tells me she is now working on the fourth floor with the hamsters, mice, and parrots, that she feeds the birds and cleans their cages. This is all new. She has apparently been judged stable enough to be given the privilege to leave the ward to work on another floor of the building. I am thrilled.

"That's a good job," I say.

"It's a tedious job. I'm working on the fourth floor, feeding the animals. I'm wearing my underwear." She shows me her bra strap. "This is me. I put my life on the line. I took a chance and I made it. I put my life on the line . . . People in glass houses shouldn't throw stones . . . Cause I love being in the hospital. It's my age . . . it's the toilet and everything . . ."

She tells me that a previous doctor of hers passed away.

"Should I worry that I might pass away, too?"

"I don't want no one to pass away on me. . . . You came all the way here to see me? Why? Because I'm well-behaved . . . I couldn't stay home. I would have ruined my reputation."

"How?"

"Hanging around in the streets, in the gutter."

She's playing with the dollar bills in her hand. We sit together silently for a while.

"The animals are talking to me. They want me to be somebody, but they don't know who I should be."

She becomes agitated and starts telling me repeatedly to take what I want in life, to take what I want.

"I'm taking a chance. I don't know what to do . . . I'm lost . . . I don't know what to do . . . I need an escort . . . it's a gorilla warfare problem . . . A male patient was bothering me and I called him a motherfucker. It'll balance out to a smooth ride. Watch my back."

She looks out at the other patients in the dayroom.

"They're going to die . . . they didn't come back . . . I'm going to be beautiful when I die. Smooth ride . . . I'm afraid I'll fall backward in the real world! I need to be locked up! I'm afraid something's going to happen to me in the outside world if I'm not locked up! My identification is coming back to me . . . the accelerator . . . it's coming back to me—flashbacks, backflashes, dreams . . ."

"Of what?"

"Jumping down the tracks, drowning on the beach, taking a knife and cutting . . . I can't go home and carry a knife. I'm afraid of carrying a knife. I'm stuck in the knife world . . . It's not safe . . . I hid knives behind the refrigerator at home because I was afraid someone was coming to get me. I jumped into the subway tracks because I thought someone was coming after me with a knife!" She's shouting quite loudly now.

"You're responsible for my dental mouth! You're my responsibility! Do you know that?"

"I know it now."

"I took my life, you know. I jumped the track! I took my life! I jumped in the subway!"

"Why'd you do it?"

"I didn't want to live any more. You have to help me! I'm too wild! You have to help me! I'm afraid people are going to influence me—like a fish!" She makes the swimming movement of a fish with her hand. "I don't want you to go! I don't want you to go! I'm always dying somewhere!"

She pauses for a moment, looks at me, then continues.

"I see you as a man talking to me and not as a sexual object, because I don't even know what a man looks like! You have to do something about its going too fast! It's going too fast! I'm staying! I made up my mind to stay! I want to stay! Reality! It's coming fast at me!"

She pauses.

"I'm going to give you a prescription. You know, the way the doctor gives a prescription to his patient?"

She nods.

I write in my notebook: "1. Eat slowly 2. Breathe 3. Keep talking," and then read it aloud to her.

She says I should add, "Have a nice dinner, take your medicine, a gown, a ring, a bath."

I add these, tear out the page, and give it to her.

"Remember, I'm wild! You've got to take care of me!"

I tell her it's time for us to stop now, that I will see her next week. She walks me down the corridor to the door out of the ward.

"Good night, Dr. Poser, Steven, good night," she says, and blows me a kiss.

I wish her good night and lock the door behind me.

18

I come into the ward just when the patients are being taken downstairs to the courtyard. Agnes is reluctant to go outside. I offer to walk her down the stairs. "I'm taking it easy," she says. When we get outside she wants to sit with me. There's no bench free so I suggest we sit on the grass.

"You surprise me," she says when we're seated.

"If you can sit on the grass, so can I."

"You're true blue," she says.

"You're true blue," I reply.

"It's reality, I'm not losing it . . . I'm taking a nap on the grass."

She lies down on my left side and begins picking clover. A male patient comes over and joins us.

"Can I trust you?" he asks me. He's trembling and seems very apprehensive. He looks in my face and asks me to take off my glasses. "Where are we? What is this place?"

Agnes answers for me: "You're in the hospital. This is a hospital."

He seems very nervous about Agnes being there. He tells me about an incident that occurred with another patient on our ward, Lily, when they were in another building together. He says she had been drying off after she had come out of the shower and had put her arms around him while she was naked.

"I don't want to hear about it," says Agnes, then to me: "I'm not a beast, I'm a reality . . . it's over, it's over, it's over."

"What's over?"

"A condition." She shows me her shoe full of coins. She says she's saving it for socks, bras, and underwear. She tells me she was taken to the university hospital for X-rays because of a respiratory problem but that it was all right now. I ask her whether she'd like to be a college girl. She laughs.

"I just want to become a person."

"You don't have to go to college to learn that."

"I know. Bah! Humbug! Ha! Ha!"

We go back upstairs to the ward. She's playful and laughing. She says that her family didn't want to get involved. I tell her she may have to get along without them. She acknowledges this.

"It takes time," she says, "remember, remember . . . it's digging."

She makes a digging motion with her hand, then, "This is me, this is me."

"I know."

"We'll just forget about those . . . those . . . those bloody days and think about the good days . . . It's 1995."

"How many years have you been here?"

"It doesn't matter. I'm here. I'm safe."

We play a game: I draw what she asks me to in my notebook: a bunny rabbit, a cat, a horn, a tape recorder, a mouse. She laughs at the mouse and says, "You dirty rat!" Then I draw a house, a female figure, and a dog. "What else?" I ask. She asks for a sun, a moon, and a tree. Another patient comes up and wants her to go downstairs to the vending machines with her.

Agnes refuses, saying to her, "I just don't want to go off the ward. I feel anxiety and stress."

Then to me: "I'm so proud of you! I didn't get killed on the stairs! You help me . . . I'm not jumping! I'm not jumping!"

She taps me on the shoulder: "I'm home."

19

As soon as I appear in the dayroom, Agnes greets me, beaming.

"Doctor! Doctor! Come to see me! I don't need any sex! I don't have to go to the bathroom too much! I'm not a medical alert! I love you! I love you! This is me! This is me! It's me!"

"Who else could it be? It's been you all along."

"It's a small world, doctor. I love you."

She shows me her new haircut.

"See? Isn't it pretty?"

"Yes, it's very pretty."

"It's me, raindrop me!"

She starts singing "Raindrops Keep Fallin' on My Head," then, "It's over! Kool Aid! Cookies! Arts and crafts! It keeps me occupied . . . keeps me out of trouble."

It's time to go to classes.

"Doctor, what time is it?"

"Ten-thirty."

"Keep an eye on me. Keep an eye on me."

She goes off to her class.

Back in the dayroom, she continues.

"I missed you."

"I missed you, too."

"Please don't throw me away. I'm very slow at learning."

"You learn at your own pace."

"I don't want to die."

She says she's afraid of killing herself.

"Are you scared of people?"

"My mother had plenty of hatred toward me. My father's saving my life. My mother's got the razor. I'm suicidal. She's running after me. She's jealous. She wants to take all my money."

"How do you feel about that?"

"I feel hurt. I feel mentally ill. That's why I'm here. I'm mentally ill. They're wise to it. She took me in . . . no more money. 'Fuck you!' she said. She wants me dead. She's trying to kill me. I'm aware of what's going on. My grandmother's a witch with long stringy hair and veins. I know it. I have to be locked up."

"To keep you safe."

"Now you're being a doctor! My mother's a gypsy, sleeping around at night, doing dirty things."

"You mean your mother's a whore?"

"She's a whore. My mother wouldn't feed me. I can't handle it. I'm hanging on to my strength, my willpower, my love, my sanity, my peace. I want peace of mind. I want peace. People are trying to kill me . . . Samantha wants to kill me. I was so scared. I can't sleep. I feel like crying. I'm so scared."

She starts weeping, gets up, and turns toward the bathroom.

"You'll be right here?"

"I'll be right here."

She goes off to the bathroom. She comes out bawling, tears streaming down her face.

"I'm afraid! I'm afraid!" she whimpers, her voice like a helpless little child. She's standing near the entrance to the bathroom. The nurse goes over and tries to comfort her, then takes her down the corridor to the seclusion room. After a few minutes, the nurse comes over and tells me that Agnes has been off Clozaril for five days because of a problem with her liver that was discovered in doing routine blood work. In a little while, Agnes comes back into the dayroom, sits down, looks over toward me, and starts crying again. She goes down the corridor into the psychiatrist's office. She's sobbing like a baby:

"Samantha is going to hurt me! Please don't let anybody hurt me!"

20

I'm talking to Agnes in the dayroom.

"I'm going to school all my life," she says. "Arts and crafts, sewing, construction work, painting, coloring, conversation, psychiatry . . . I was crying a little bit . . . yeah."

I look down at Nicole, who's lying on the floor.

"What's she doing?" I ask Agnes.

"She's dreaming. She's dreaming about me. She's dreaming about going on a roller coaster. Fasten your seatbelt and hang on!"

"Did you ever go on a roller coaster?"

"I fell out of a roller coaster. I went flying into the sky. My mother got hurt. My mother and father got hurt. That's why I'm so nervous."

"Are you all right now?"

"Yeah. My mother got hurt, flying through the air."

She falls silent and looks over at the TV for a few minutes.

"I have to go pee pee," she says, then gets up and goes to the bathroom. It's locked. She goes over to the garbage pail and looks through it. She comes back and sits down, waggling her foot. She takes my notebook and tries to read. I ask her if she would like to write something. She writes, "Peace be with you, Steven Poser, and Happy Thanksgiving to you every day. Love, Agnes."

She gives it to me.

"Thank you."

"It's a little poem. It's ten o'clock. I don't know."

"What don't you know?"

"I don't know what I'm doing."

Silence.

"It's nice to have a roof over your head when you're in trouble," she continues.

"A safe roof."

"I'm hungry."

"What do you think they're having for lunch?"

"Mashed potatoes, salad, soup . . . you're writing a story."

"The story of my life, . . . and you're helping."

She smiles.

"How's the house?"

"It's fine."

"What color?"

"White."

I tell her about putting a bag of garbage outside, hearing a big disturbance that night, and going out to discover a raccoon rummaging through it. She smiles.

"That's cute, . . . I don't know . . ."

She looks over at the TV. It's showing people fighting.

"I don't like this picture," she says.

She gets up and turns off the TV. She comes back.

"Too much fighting," I say.

"I can't stand it," she says.

21

"I'm going to play Bingo at one thirty," says Agnes, "I'm going to win!"

"You're winning all the time."

"I died. The good and the bad . . . right down to the nitty gritty . . . Judgement Day . . . I'm stuck here . . . I waited 'til the last minute . . . I want to get there, too . . . I want action! See? I want action! I died! I came back! When the dentist comes around! I jumped in the train tracks! I had Holy water! Holy Communion! And you know what happened? I got a second chance in my life! You know this is me! Surprised?"

"I know this is you."

"The nurse is very smart, she got a patient she can trust."

The dayroom is filled with the sound of overlapping voices, yelling, and screams. Everybody's acting up at once.

"And I'll tell you one thing," she continues, "I'm not coming home with no man!"

"Why's that?"

"I'm not laying around in bed with no man!"

She breaks into raucous laughter.

"No, you're playing it safe."

"I'm the safest one here, I'm tickled pink! I'm so happy I made it through! You know who your friends are when you come back!"

She goes off to play Bingo.

22

It's time to go outside for a smoking break. I walk down the stairs with Agnes. She seems fine with it. She's wearing a turquoise, pink, and blue ski parka. I tell her what a nice jacket she has on. She thanks me. I ask her what she's planning to have for Thanksgiving. "Turkey, stuffing, pumpkin pie . . . Thank you, Doctor." When we get to the bottom, she goes off into the courtyard. The next time I see her, she's with Timothy, a small, gnomelike man whom I have often seen spitting on his hand and then rubbing it on the top of his head from front to back, repeating this movement over and over. I have never heard him speak, though he has approached me several times very shyly, touched my hand softly, then withdrew. Agnes and Timothy are walking together slowly by themselves, arm in arm, pressed close to each other. He's smoking a cigarette and giving her drags, which she takes, though I have never seen her smoking before. The nurse calls all the female patients to get in line to go back inside the building. Agnes and Timothy come toward the line, still arm in arm. She separates from him, strokes his face softly several times, then kisses her hand and plants it on his cheek. She gets in line and begins to go up the stairs, but turns twice to look directly back at him. I think I see a tear fall from her eye before she disappears up the stairwell. I am nearly moved to tears myself—it's the first expression of tenderness from her toward another human being I have ever witnessed.

Back upstairs on the ward, she comes bursting into the dayroom and heads directly toward me.

"You don't know what you're missing!"

"What?"

"Garter belts! White support hose! Yarmulkes! Ha! Ha! Ha! Play the game! Two pairs of underwear! Don't you get it?"

She looks over at Samantha, who is laughing her head off by the windows.

"She's laughing at me over there!" says Agnes.

"What for?"

"She thinks I'm a clown!"

She breaks out into raucous laughter.

"It's a riot in here," I say.

"You should see what it looks like at night! Some bullshit! Where's the gobble gobble turkey? You're an Easter Bunny, where's the turkey?"

More laughter.

"I'm going to work!" she exclaims.

Samantha is meanwhile talking furiously into the air by the window. Agnes is overflowing with hilarious laughter watching Samantha.

"It's a funny picture!" she squeals, then, "Turquoise! Your garter belt!"

23

Agnes is sitting by the door inside the dayroom. She's got both hands full of coins.

"I like myself," she says, "it's an acrobatic balance. I had open heart surgery. I woke up brand new. I'm not reality. I'm getting my feet on the ground."

She puts both her hands filled with coins into her pockets.

"I'm forty-six years old. I need a bathroom . . . Precious moment, tender moment, tender moment, right? Excuse me."

She goes off, saying, "I'm taking a walk."

She walks around the dayroom. She comes back.

"I like staying my distance. I'm feeling good. They took three tubes of pitch-black blood out of me. Do you like my blouse?"

It's white with blue polka dots and red stripes.

"Yes, I like it very much."

"I've got a whole closet full of new clothes, I started a new life when I got here."

Joanna, who has been sitting in the corner behind us the whole time, now turns on her portable radio. The antenna is broken and someone has stolen her earphones. The radio is tuned between two stations, producing an irritating mixed signal with a lot of static.

"Like the radio," Agnes says, "I think it's trouble."

"I'd like to throw it out the window," I say.

"It's demanding, it's continuous, it's repetitious . . . Psst, this is me! There is no problem! This is me! There is no problem! I'm intelligent! Darkness, the hour of darkness. This is me, my hour of darkness. I'm very smart. I know how to put my foot there or not there. I know how to put on a shoe, you know what I mean? I know how to take my own life but not take other peoples' lives. I get along with the people here. Some of them can get a little mean. I still get along with them. See? I like to be protected . . . bodyguards, you know. I had peaches, apple cider . . . I don't believe in sexual intercourse after you're not sick any more. I like my family. It all depends on what kind of men you go out with."

"What kind of men?"

"West Point men. I promised a decorated life, but there's a catch to it. I kept my promise."

"What is it?"

"To *be* there . . . it's the men I go out with . . . I like college men . . . it's the men I associate with . . . Promise me . . . Promise me . . ."

"I promise."

"I'm very lucky! The men aren't taking care of these wild women; they're taking care of *me!* I know what's going on, Doctor Poser. I know what I'm doing! Do you know the Ape House at the zoo? There's a reason! I have beautiful taste in clothes."

"You certainly do."

"It's all because of my mother and father! I love my mother and father . . . and they'll jump the gun . . . what they did! They jumped the gun! I'm a woman! I kept my promise! I kept my promise!"

She's become quite agitated. She gets up and walks to a table at the other end of the dayroom. She comes back.

"I'm back."

"You've been back for a while; it's a miracle, really."

"Timmy, Mark, Johnny, Steven, it's the men, the men I associate with . . . See, there's a war going on! You're back! You will! You're living! You're not bumping off!"

"You're living."

"Yes, my nails are growing . . . no more picking."

"Thank goodness."

"I'm not missing anything, you know. I'm not missing nothing! I'm a very lucky girl . . . woman. I've got a bloody angel on my shoulder. I'm under control, I'm trying to say! I've got men controlling me. I'm going back to work, but not yet. I'm too young, not yet."

24

Agnes comes and sits down next to me.

"I made it. I don't know who, where, or what, but I'm not sitting in any man's lap in the vending machines room!"

She's very angry, apparently at something she saw going on downstairs.

"Stripping off all her clothes! Feeling themselves up! This is a psychiatric hospital! If they think I'm going to pay their bills around here, they're nuts! They'll have to cut my hand off! I'm not giving you my fucking money! . . . You know something, Doctor Poser? I'm not a welfare patient! I'm not sitting in the vending machine room in no man's lap! I'm not a bum! I died! I wish they would leave me the hell alone! I don't get it! You're full of shit! I don't get it! I work harder than you! You're talking to the wrong people! They sit on their asses waiting for a handout! You're talking to the wrong people! They don't give a shit! . . . If you don't get it by now, you never will! My mother and father come first and the rest of you can go fuck yourselves! I died! Black blood! I came back!"

She's yelling into the dayroom now, instead of at me.

"You better leave me the fuck alone! Lay the hell off! See what's going on? I fed my dog Lester! I fed my cat! My family! You can go to hell!"

"I've been talking to the wrong people," I say.

"Whores! Lesbians! Hookers! Bums! I'm telling you, Doctor, you're talking to the wrong people! These girls smother you in your bed at night!"

We're quiet for a while.

"I have my reasons. I'm taking care of myself, just because I want my mother and father to be all right. Thank you for talking to me . . . My folks want me locked up! And I love every minute of it because I love my stinking mother and father! I'm going to be a patient all my life and I don't get it! Bum! Feelings! In other words, I'm a patient, I'm not a gypsy!"

Samantha comes over.

Agnes says to her: "I used your soap, I used your shampoo. Forgive me. I'm forty-six years old. I used your underwear."

"I thought you flushed it down the toilet," says Samantha.

Agnes, now back to me: "I'm forty-six. I'm very lucky. I have a roof over my head and a toilet bowl. Yeah, you understand. Pressure, inside and outside. I had to let it out."

"You did the right thing."

"This is me. This is me, Doctor. Too much pressure. Too much pressure. You understand. I pulled them under a tidal wave! A tidal wave on the ocean! I pulled through!"

"It's very important what you say."

"A miracle happened! Like a miracle, like a new woman . . . I walked in and it was . . . I was . . . I feel depressed that I did . . . You know what? I'm the middle of a war!"

25

A week before Christmas. It's snowing outside. I go over to Agnes. She's talking about what they're going to serve for lunch. She's concerned about my driving a car when it's snowing.

"Did I tell you what happened?" she asks. "A wire came out of the Christmas tree. I remember swallowing something. I didn't know what it was. Christmas tree wire. It came out in the toilet, Steven. A wire caught in my stomach. It came out of me. I was so upset when I saw it. I told the doctor. He said okay. I'm telling the truth, Doctor."

"I believe you."

"I'm very lucky. I know I'm in the hospital. I know what's going on. Electrical wire. I swallowed it. I'm OK now. It came out. You have a lot to do with it. You sit with me and I don't budge. I made it. I'm serious, Doctor. I'm lucky. I'm very fortunate to have my life saved. I worked so hard. That's why they keep giving me prune juice. I love sleeping. I love sleeping."

"You slept all morning."

"I enjoy my life. I love sleeping. I love eating. I like prune juice . . . I hated getting out of bed. Boy, did I hate getting out of bed this morning! Do you like me?"

"What do you think?"

"Yeah, . . . I've got a good reputation. I'm no prostitute. . . . When I swallowed that wire, I was so upset. This is a hospital, right,

Steven? Right? . . . Do you have a girlfriend? That you go home to? That doesn't cheat on you?"

"What about you?"

"I don't know any men."

"Do you want a boyfriend?"

"I can't find a boyfriend!" She laughs. "I can't find a boyfriend! I want a husband to bring me presents on my birthday! It's twenty-five to four . . . the hour of my lifespan . . . boredom . . . I live here . . . I don't know . . . I live here . . . I live here . . . Are you going to see her when you go home?"

26

Agnes is sitting in her chair by the door into the dayroom. She's wearing white pants and a polka dot shirt. She wants to tell me something.

"I was in a wheelchair. I collapsed in the rehab building. My legs gave way. I went down head first."

"What happened?"

"I'm a patient. I ate my lunch. I'm a patient. It hurts. I'm for real. I collapsed in a wheelchair. I'm for real. I couldn't get up."

"Did that ever happen to you before?"

"Yes, it did."

She calls over to the nurse: "Nurse, I'm having trouble breathing."

Then back to me: "It hurts, you know, it hurts."

I'm not sure what she's telling me. She says her birthday's coming up, March 18. She'll be forty-seven. I ask her if she'd like me to remember that. She says she would. I write it down in my notebook. She goes over to the TV and turns down the volume. She comes back and sits down.

"I don't like noise," she says.

I'm slumping in my chair, just like her. She sits up. I sit up.

"Sit up straight," she says, "that's what they tell you . . . are you getting old?"

"Yeah, I'm getting to be an old man. How about you?"

She shows me her hair, says it's turning grey.

I tell her I talked to Dr. Hartman today, that I'll be here till May and then I'll be leaving.

"Oh. What'll happen to Barney?"

"He'll stay here with Dr. Kurtz."

"I fell head first in the rehab building two days ago; they had to bring me back to the ward in a wheelchair."

"Are the drugs making you dizzy?"

"No. Too much stress. The job is too hard. I'm not going to the program. They force me. I'm intelligent. They lock me up. I'm smart . . . I feel very sick. I'm very, very sick."

She starts nodding off.

"I'm tired," she says.

"Want to lie down?"

"Yes."

"Here, put your head here," I say, pointing to the cushion of her chair.

She lies down on her side with her knees up to her chest, her hands tucked under her head.

"Good night, Steven."

"Good night, Agnes."

"Good night, Steven."

I sit with her while she sleeps.

After a while, she wakes up, sweaty and groggy.

"You're up," I say.

"I'm sick," she replies.

She starts whimpering and sobbing to herself. After a bit of this she asks me if she can go lie down in the observation room. The nurse comes over. She tells me that Agnes fell down in the rehab program, that they brought her back in a wheelchair, and that once she got back to the ward she was walking all right.

Agnes wails: "Help me! Help me, Doctor!"

I get her up on her feet and the nurse takes her off to the observation room.

When I see her next, she is again sitting by the door into the dayroom, rocking from the waist with her hands gripping the arms of her chair. In her white pants and polka dot shirt, she looks like a circus clown, a tragic Pierrot. I tell her I'll see her next week and leave the ward.

27

"It's my choice," says Agnes, "I don't want to go out. It's getting dangerous out there. All is well. All is well. I'm going to lay me down. I died and came back! They operated on me! I flew in the sky upside down! I flew in the sky upside down! I made it! You and the doctors and the staff must have done something right! I made it! I came back! You know what? I feel good! I'm happy today! I'm proud of you! You did your job! I'm not anxious today! It's my life, right? My life! They saved my life! I had chocolate pudding, Pepsi Cola, ice cream sandwich, roll and butter, chocolate pudding! . . . I'm young people. I've been locked up 'til I grow tall, be an adult. I want to be sure. It's too fast out there—carburetors, motors, cars . . . I have to be sure."

She gets up to get a cup of prune juice the nurse has brought in for her. Nicole comes over and sits down beside me. Agnes comes back with her prune juice.

"Excuse me!" she yells at Nicole. "Up, twat! Get up, twat!"

Nicole gets up and goes off. Agnes sits down in the chair.

"What was that name you called her?"

"Twat, Miss Twat," she replies.

"Not a very nice name."

"I came back alive. Thank you. I came back alive. I died and came back."

"Welcome back."

She sees another patient throw half a cheese sandwich into the garbage pail and goes over to retrieve it. She stuffs it into her mouth. Then she goes to the nurse's table and gets a container of yogurt. She comes back and sits down.

"I need it," she says, stirring the yogurt.

"What flavor?"

"Blueberry."

"Excuse me," she says, "please let me eat this."

"Eat it," I say.

She eats it.

"Excuse me," she says.

She gets up to take the empty cup to the garbage pail. She goes off to the bathroom. When she comes out, she sits down near the bathroom door.

28

"Doctor, do you smell paint?"

"Yes, they're working on the second floor."

"OK."

She gets up. She sits down again, four chairs away, waggling the foot of her crossed leg, holding herself across the chest, then putting her hands through the cuffs and into the sleeves on the opposite side.

"I want pizza. I'm saving my money. I'm forty-six, you know what I mean?"

"What do you mean?"

"I've got a stomach ache. I'm forty-six years old. A man came to ask me to come back to work when I feel better. The dentist, . . . Maalox . . . 'Come to the apartment,' he said. I don't want to sit around all day like a stick. . . . There's nothing out there for me! I'm not missing nothing!"

She falls silent.

She shows me her thumb, which looks like it's healing from having the nail ripped off.

"Factory work, my reputation, right?"

She's got several handfuls of coins in her shirt pocket. She takes them out.

"I changed all my money in the dollar bill machine. A man came up to me in the vending machines and asked to kiss me. 'You may *not!*' I said, and I ran away. He thought he was a wise guy! . . . It was bothering me."

"Thank you for telling me."

"I have to go to the bathroom, please excuse me."

"You're excused."

She goes off.

She comes back, handling her coins.

"I'm saving it! It's me! It's me! It's me! This is me! This is me!"

She opens her eyes wide and stares at me.

"What are we going to do about you?"

She smiles, her eyes still wide.

"I don't know," she says.

She falls silent.

"This is me! This is me! This is me! You're very smart, you're very smart."

"Thank you."

"This is me! This is me! I flew over! I flew over! I flew over!"

"Like a bird?"

"Like an airplane! I flew over! I flew over! Bath! Shower! The dentist! Cecilia Street! My mother and father's house! The bedroom! Purple bedspread! Gold lamp! My parents! Velvet drapes! It's too late for that nonsense! Too late for that nonsense! Too late for that nonsense!"

"Is it too late for me, too?"

"It's an old record . . . Yeah, it's too late for that . . . stripping . . . I have to go the bathroom."

She gets up and goes off.

29

I ask Agnes how she spent the weekend. She says she had a good time. She had Chinese food in the basement cafeteria, egg rolls and noodles.

"I know what I'm doing; I came here for the money."

"You're well-paid, well-groomed, well-dressed, and well-fed."

"I know what I'm doing. I got Yoo-hoo chocolate drink."

There's a hairdresser on the ward giving haircuts to any of the patients who want one.

Agnes gets up to watch. All of a sudden, she collapses on the floor near where the hairdresser is working. Her legs seem to give way and she falls backwards, banging her head against a radiator. I'm there immediately. She's a bit dazed, but not hurt.

"I'm not feeling well," she says. "I collapsed. I'm sorry about that."

"You don't have to apologize."

"Something's bothering me . . . the package never came . . . I'm going flying in the sky . . . I feel sick . . ."

"I shouldn't have let you fall."

Her voice in reply keeps shifting between an anguished cry for help, furious indignation, and wistful resignation:

". . . please take care of me . . . too much pressure, the doctor, money, the dog . . . I don't get it! This is a hospital! I collapsed! I don't feel good . . . that's my story—I fall down wherever I go . . . I wasn't expecting it. Everywhere I go it happens. Everywhere I go."

30

A male rehab therapist comes into the dayroom with a great flourish, his voice booming. He goes around the room greeting several patients. He's got a package. He goes to Agnes and gives it to her. She opens it. It's a big box of Peeps—yellow marshmallow Easter candies in the shape of baby chicks. She thanks him, puts the box on her lap and holds it with both hands. Everybody's watching.

"I hate this place," says Mrs. Lutzky.

Agnes refuses to give away any of the Peeps. She takes the box off to the far corner of the dayroom and settles in to eat the whole thing. I go over and sit next to her.

"We get our money today," she says, "eight dollars. It's my life. It's my life."

She proceeds to eat the whole box, stuffing one Peep after another into her mouth until they're all gone. She's got granulated sugar all over her hands and face and down the front of her shirt.

"I need it," she says, in between swallowing. "Looks like I made it. I'm surprised." Then she gets up, goes off to the bathroom, comes out, and sits down on the opposite side of the room.

31

Agnes comes over with two packages of Oreo cookies and offers me some. Another patient comes and tries to get some, too.

"Leave me alone!" Agnes bursts out and shoos her away.

"I saved a woman's life this afternoon. She didn't fall backwards on the stairs and get killed. She started to fall and I grabbed her and saved her. I saved a woman's life this afternoon! I saved a woman's life this afternoon! I saved a woman's life this afternoon!"

"I'm proud of you."

"I fell out of the roller coaster, parachute jump! My mother saved my life! I went flying in the air! She caught me! Saved my life! I saw the picture through! I made it!"

We sit together in silence for a while.

"It's getting time for me to be going soon," I say.

"Take care of yourself, meatballs and spaghetti, mashed potatoes, cold soda, prune juice . . ."

She looks at me very directly.

"What are you writing?"

I show her the notebook. She looks at what I just wrote.

"Prune juice?"

"What should I write?"

She dictates:

"Please come to me tomorrow. Pay. Love, Agnes. Eight dollars. Please pay your bill. Thank you."

I write all this down, then tell her I will see her next week. I leave the dayroom.

32

Agnes is in a wheelchair. She's got bandages around her ankle. I go over to her.

"What happened to you?"

"I fell in the dayroom. Hit my head. I flew in the sky. I died! They gave me two white pills and I came back to life. . . . I don't feel well. I'm very upset. Claire kicked me."

She shows me her shin.

"Are you still bringing pizza?" she asks.

"In about three weeks."

"Will you still come to see us?"

"I'd like to try."

"I have to go to the bathroom. Will you excuse me?"

She goes off in the wheelchair. In a few minutes, she comes back.

"Can you get in the elevator in that thing?" I ask her.

"No," she says, "I'm going to stay in."

"When did you fall?"

"Yesterday . . . you weren't here."

"Do you think you would have fallen if I'd been here?"

"No. I fell because you weren't here, Steven. I'm feeling a little better now. I'm making it. I'm going for a ride."

"See you later, alligator."

"In a while, crocodile."

She goes off in the wheelchair.

33

The dayroom is sleepy and quiet. Agnes is sitting across the room, examining her nails and yawning. She looks toward me. She picks some crumbs off the front of her blouse, gets up, tries to get into the bathroom but it's locked. She gets the therapy aide to let her in. She goes in, flushes the toilet, and comes out. She comes over to me.

"How was lunch?" I ask.

"Mashed potatoes, spinach, peaches . . . not coffee—too much caffeine for a schizophrenic. You like my blouse? This is me! Roller coaster, parachute jump, barrel of fun, hot dogs, knishes . . . This is me! New Year's resolution! Egg nog, saltwater taffy . . . dentist needle *this* big! Scared! Drink hot chocolate. Drink it slow. I'm not going nowhere. I got paid. I'm a lucky stiff! I'm not going nowhere! See? Control! See? (she shows me her finger) Pierced! Sewing machine. My mother and father got mad at me." She giggles, then continues: "Barricini chocolate cherries. Don't go down the stairs any more. I only go in the elevator. You picked me up and carried me. Saved my life. I remember that. I appreciate that."

"I appreciate that you remember."

"It's too dangerous to go down there. Strangers. I got scared. I got sick. I died. I came back to life and had an answer."

"What was the answer?"

"Freedom! I got my freedom! My mother and father used to drink a lot of whiskey. . . . toothache . . . Please come back."

"I'll be back."

I go downstairs. Mrs. Lutzky is eating a candy bar. She tells me her father and her brother got thrown into the lion's den at the Bronx Zoo. She says that if you chew gum under water you can breathe under water. I buy a chocolate milk and a candy bar for Agnes and go back upstairs.

I give Agnes the chocolate milk and the candy bar. She starts eating.

"I paid all my bills. I laid me down for my problem. The budget was handled so beautifully, and I didn't get hurt . . . you know why . . . you be my friend, I'll be your friend."

I write the words, "Name," "Date," and "Message" in my notebook and give it to her.

She writes: "Happy Mother's Day, Steven. Happy New Year to you, Dr. Poser."

She gives the notebook back.

"You know my mother and father's joy is me! Not backstabbing! Not stabbing them in the back! I had an operation . . . set up a school . . . push people . . . babysitting. I'll tell you one thing. I'm not a gypsy! That's for sure! I'm not a gypsy! I fell into a swamp. I had to start all over again. I had to repeat myself. I fell in a swamp on Cecilia Street. I had to start a new life again. You understand what I'm talking about. I fell. I had to start a new life again. I couldn't make it. I jumped in the subway. I had my life spared by a fraction of a second. The Police Department knows me."

Denise comes by, singing, "*Don't make me over / Now that I'd do anything for you / Don't make me over / Now that you know how I adore you / . . .*"

"I'm honest," says Agnes, "it's twenty-five to four."

Mrs. Lutzky is ordering Chinese food out of the air:

". . . fried wonton, Chinese spare ribs, lobster Cantonese, shrimp chow mein, roast pork, spring rolls, dim sum, sweet and sour pork . . ."

Agnes continues: "Doctor, see? It fits . . . I'm forty-six years old and it fits."

Mrs. Lutzky is still ordering food out of the air: ". . . sweet and sour chicken, bok choy, broccoli with garlic sauce, beef lo mein, pork lo mein, fried shrimp toast, sweet and sour shrimp, tomato egg drop soup, wonton soup, pepper steak, fried rice, egg rolls, shrimp rolls, moo shoo pork . . ."

Agnes interrupts, saying, "Steven, it's in the book."

It's time for me to go.

"Drink hot chocolate," she says, "go to the dentist and come back."

"See you next week," I say.

34

In the vending machines area, I buy a package of potato chips for Agnes. Upstairs again, I go over to where she's sitting by the windows and give it to her.

"You saved a life," she exclaims. "It's the potato chips! It's the potato chips! Thank you, Doctor! It's my life! My life is on the line! Her life is on the line, right this minute! Her life is on the line right this minute! Doctor, her life was on the line! Her life! Her life!"

She's finished eating the potato chips and is looking at my shoes. "Polish your shoes?"

"Yes."

"Esquire shoe polish, right?"

"Right; what kind of shoes do you have?"

"Buster Brown sneakers."

"Good."

The therapy aide calls over to me from across the room: "Next week's going to be your last?"

"Yes," I reply.

"Boy, am I going to miss you," says Agnes.

"I'm going to miss you, too."

"You know, Doctor, I don't know too many people in this world. Just me and you . . . Where you going?"

"Right now, I'm going home, but I'll be back next week."

"Can I walk you to the door?"
She walks me down the corridor in silence.
"Goodnight, Steven."
"Goodnight, Agnes."

35

The last day.

As I enter the dayroom, Agnes is sitting by the door.

"I went to the bathroom. I'm looking forward to having a slice of pizza this afternoon. I'll be right here. I died in the dorm room last night. I fell and hit my head. I've got eight dollars. I've got all my money."

"You don't have to fall down to get paid," I tell her. "You'll get that money for the rest of your life. You've got a pension."

"I've gotta walk," she says, and goes off.

She comes back holding a string of beads.

"You want them? I threw them in the garbage. Who needs beads in the hospital? I fell down. I lost my balance. I don't feel well."

"I want you to feel safe."

"What are you writing?"

"I don't know. I started a word and now I can't remember what it was. I get lost, but I come back again, just like you."

She coughs.

"I gotta walk," she says, and goes off.

It's time for the party. The therapy aide announces that we're all going outside now for pizza and that everyone should line up in the corridor. Everyone leaves the dayroom except Agnes. She's sitting at a table in the far corner all by herself. I go over.

"Coming to the party?"

"I'm afraid to leave."

"I'll go with you."

"You go with me so I don't fall . . . you have to help me."

"OK."

She gets up and we leave the dayroom. All the patients are lined up in the corridor. The elevator's broken. We have to take the stairs, three flights down. Agnes gets panicky.

"I'll walk you down," I say, "we'll go real slow, one step at a time. Hold on to the rail, you won't fall."

I offer her my hand. She looks at me querulously and takes it. We're at the front of the line, the two of us, going down one step at a time, holding hands. At several points, she stops and sharply demands, "Don't push me!" Once we're down to the bottom, I lead her out of the building and she goes along with the other patients toward the picnic area. There's a large open-air gazebo with benches and tables inside. Most of the patients sit there. Dr. Hartman and several other staff people join us. The delivery man from Lombardi's is waiting in a Jeep. He's got twelve pizzas packed in two large insulated carriers. We've also got a dozen liter bottles of soda in assorted flavors. All this gets set up on picnic tables just outside the gazebo. When everything's ready, the patients start passing by the picnic tables and dig in. There's not much talk. They get their food and eat it. I'm standing around talking to various staff people. Agnes has already had three slices. We're down to the last pie. She takes a fourth slice. It's getting to be time to start cleaning up. Dr. Hartman and I break down all the cardboard pizza boxes and put them in a big plastic garbage bag.

Agnes comes up to me.

"Thank you. Thank you. Soda. . . . Every time I go somewhere and feel like I'm falling down, you'll be there, right?"

"Right."

"Thank you."

I take both her hands in mine and look very directly and openly into her eyes. We connect. After a moment, she turns and goes back inside the building.

PART II
Mrs. Lutzky

1

First contact, my second week on the ward.

The nurse is giving a class called Mental and Physical Health. The topic for discussion is "Mind and Body." The nurse is telling the patients that they have both a mind and a body.

Hilary: "I'm a mind without a body."

Mrs. Lutzky, an older-looking woman with a thick Yiddish accent, confronts me from across the room: "Why don't you strangle me for good? Throw me out the window!" She continues exclaiming to me about Moe in Williamsburg, how they serve schnapps in the restaurants, that the food here is poisoned and they put bleach in the shampoo and that's why her hair is ruined.

Lucia, a dark-haired woman sitting on the opposite side of the room, also addresses me directly for the first time: "I know you. You're the professor from Heidelberg. You're Professor Heidelberg." She seems very pleased to recognize me.

Mrs. Lutzky continues bursting out at me: "Why don't you just throw me out the window? I know you! You killed my mother! Broke her bones! You're a human meat grinder! You and Moe! Everybody wants to be a Hitler! You'll get yours! You'll die like an animal!"

This continues for about five minutes.

"Thanks a lot," I say to her.

Nurse (to Mrs. Lutzky): "That's not a very nice thing to say. Dr. Poser is our new psychology intern. He's going to be with us for a while."

Mrs. Lutzky: "Alright already. I'm sorry, okay?"

She drifts off.

2

I pass by Mrs. Lutzky, who addresses me by name. She asks whether I got the Rolex she gave me the money to buy for myself, and tells me they make them with diamonds now. I tell her I'm still looking for the right one. I ask her whether I can sit down. She's enthusiastic about this.

"Cold tea. Everybody should have a cold drink with ice in it. No more water pills, Doctor. All I do is run to the bathroom. Piss and piss all day long. I'm even pissing on the floor. They hate me here. They're jealous of me. I'm the richest woman in the world. They shoot me with rock salt, poison, Oil of Olay. Everything's for them. They take all the best for them. They rob me and they hang me . . . I gave birth to a bird, a pullet bird. The most beautiful bird you've ever seen. My sister did too. She loved her bird. She washed it, dressed it, made nice soup for it to eat. Mine she doesn't feed. She gives it cold dirty water to eat."

3

Mrs. Lutzky says that they've injected all kinds of poisons into her—cyanide, arsenic, strychnine—that she's a poisoned girl.

"They want me to die. They're jealous. They want to see me dead."

She tells me that if she could get sunflower seeds she'd live forever.

"How long do you think you're going to live?"

"Maybe three months."

Another patient comes walking by, eating sunflower seeds. I ask her if those are sunflower seeds. She says yes. I ask her whether she would give one to Mrs. Lutzky. She offers a seed to Mrs. Lutzky, who refuses to take it. Mrs. Lutzky goes on talking to me. She says that she gave birth to a beautiful turkey bird and that she did all kinds of things to take care of it. It comes to her window at night and gets into bed with her.

"I knitted sweaters for him," she tells me. She says she invented various kinds of machines and also invented penicillin, but other people took the credit for it. Then she tells me she was married to Adolf Hitler. She ironed his shirts, made soup, cleaned the house. She says that at home he was a nice guy. Then she pauses, looks pensive, and says, "It'll come . . . I remember my childhood, going to school . . . I don't remember making all those machines, going to Red China." She says that the patient who offered her the sunflower seed (now gone off) came into her room and took bones out of her back with a razor blade and cut her in front (she shows me a small scab on her stomach) and burned her 'down there' with cigarettes. I ask her why people do these terrible things to her and she says they're jealous, that she's the richest woman in the world, and they're a bunch of mean bitches who like nothing better than to do you in.

4

Mrs. Lutzky greets me as soon as I come into the dayroom. She takes an earring out of her pocket and shows it to me. She tells me that the stone in it is a real gemstone. She says she wants to make a necklace out of it to wear around her neck. I tell her that's a good idea.

Agnes is walking around in a leisurely, alert sort of way, seemingly calm and controlled, none of the extreme behavior I have observed over the past two weeks. She sees me with Mrs. Lutzky, acknowledges me, and continues moving—into the bathroom, out into the dayroom, and back again. Mrs. Lutzky notices me watching Agnes.

"Agnes is a very sick girl. They really did a job on her, tore her vulva out of her. They put earthworms up there, acid. They put a rotgut needle up her vagina." She shifts abruptly to talking about herself. She says that people do all these terrible things to her because she's the richest woman in the world. She points out another patient who cut her with razors and put mustard seeds in her bed. "She killed my bird," she says. "That bird saved my life. I gave birth to this bird. They have the same sexual organs we have. My father never loved me. I had to buy his love. He liked my cousin Sadie. He makes believe he loves me but he never did."

While we're talking, another patient comes over.

"You've got a fever," she says to Mrs. Lutzky, "you're all flushed."

She touches Mrs. Lutzky's forehead lightly with her hand. Mrs. Lutzky erupts at the touch: "Don't touch me! You play with yourself all day and touch me with that hand!"

The other patient moves away quickly. Mrs. Lutzky is furious.

To the patient: "Take your filthy dirty hands off me!"

To me: "She touched a rutabaga plant!"

To the patient: "If you ever touch me like that again I'm going to kill you!"

To me: "They put a tube up my vagina and my asshole! They put acid up there! They put dirt!" More calmly now: "I'm not getting along with them. They want to kill me. Did you get the Rolex yet? You're my doctor. You know what I think? They're psychotic here. Every one of them killed at least ten people."

Agnes comes over.

Mrs. Lutzky: "You're a very sick girl, Agnes. Your vagina's coming out of your asshole."

Agnes, defiantly: "It is not!"

Agnes looks at me, indicates Mrs. Lutzky with her eyes, gets a serious look, and taps the side of her head with a finger, as though to say, "Don't listen to her, she's nuts."

5

Mrs. Lutzky tells me that her brother Morris is dying in the hospital, that they hit him with a car, and that they did this because it's better for them. She tells me there's a patient here who puts earthworms down her throat when she's asleep.

"No one cried worse than my father and mother. It was a *meshuggenah* family." I ask her who was in it. She talks about her brother Morris, her father Irving, and her mother.

Lucia is sitting nearby, praying softly with her eyes closed. She gets up and starts walking past us. She says, "I'm a baby. Okay. All right, I know. Each baby got each cell. To get out of that crazy house and land in heaven . . ." She continues walking about the dayroom in an agitated state.

Mrs. Lutzky is now waving her hands in the air and ordering Chinese food as though she were talking on the telephone: ". . . egg rolls, spring rolls, shrimp lo mein, pepper steaks, lobster Cantonese . . . There's still plenty of food left . . . Everything on the menu . . ."

She interrupts this to address me directly: "Did you get the Rolex yet? What's your name again?"

"Dr. Poser."

She tells me to get the Rolex with the diamond digital. She then continues ordering more food.

"We'll have it before twelve o'clock? Thank you."

She resumes talking to me again. "I can't walk the stairs anymore. What they did to my brother! The Chinese food was no good. I'm getting sandwiches—roast beef, turkey, pastrami—from that store near Flatbush. Boy, do I want a cigarette! Let's get out of here!"

She goes out for a while. The next time I see her she's back in the dayroom. She's bending over toward a sunlit window, holding her dress up in front. She maintains this trancelike posture for several minutes. Then she turns around and starts ordering more food out of the air. "There's a shortage of Chinese food," she says, "all kinds of spring rolls, fortune cookies, wonton soup, lo mein, pepper steak, . . . charge it to my account. How much? Three o'clock? Plenty of food. Thank you."

Lucia is crouching on the floor beneath the window by the baseboard: "Those aren't rats and mice; those are babies."

Mrs. Lutzky comes and sits down. She asks me if I know how to make cinnamon toast. I ask her to tell me. She gives detailed instructions. She also tells me how to make potato balls with chopped meat inside.

"I like you," she says, "you're charming."

"You like talking," I say.

She starts telling me about Arnie, a guy she used to know. "Now he's in trouble," she says, "he's got an Elephant Man tumor. I'm taking care of his girlfriends in the mental hospital. What a *schmuck!* I think I got a tumor also in my head. They scraped it out with a needle."

"Why'd they save you?"

"I know, I know; it's hard to figure out sometimes."

She starts ordering more food: "Lox and bagels, sturgeon, whitefish with onions, roast beef, wonton soup, steak au jus, a case of soda, cheesecake, a big chocolate cake, egg rolls with Saucy Susan. You know, I invented Saucy Susan. I also invented the Jeep. Did you know I was a doctor when I was three years old? I saved my father's eye from an iron sliver he got from welding. My mother scared the hell out of me when she caught me making love when I was fourteen years old. If I woulda told her she woulda blew a gasket!"

The radio is playing Bob Dylan, "Like a Rolling Stone." Several patients are singing along. Mrs. Lutzky is talking into the air to her brother Morris in the hospital: "I'm sending you a gallon of ice cream and a warm robe. You want a turkey drumstick with cranberry sauce? You got your teeth? You can eat that? All right. So you'll eat the Chinese food first and then the deli."

6

Mrs. Lutzky comes over.

"Doctor, my uncle's mad at me."

"I don't blame him."

"What for?"

"You can always find some reason."

"They made me brain-dead! They dumped a bottle of shampoo on my head with bird shit in it, coal tar, acid! My uncle wants me to write a will and give him all my money!"

"Why are you so nice to people who are so mean to you?"

"They might kill me. My father loved my cousin Sadie more than he loved me. She gave me a dog-brain . . . Doctor, can you get me something to eat from the nurses' room? I'm starving."

"You think I can just walk in there and bring you food just like that?"

"Please."

"I think you better wait 'til dinner time."

"Can I have a dollar? I want to go buy something from the vending machines."

"You know I don't give out money in here. Anyway, I gave all my money to the Salvation Army."

"You did?"

"You know how they stand on the corner and make a lot of noise?"

"Yeah."

"Well, I paid them just to shut up."

She laughs.

"You're such a good doctor."

"I am? I don't give you money, I don't give you food, I'm not do-ing *bubkes* here for you!"

"I'm going to get something to eat in the cafeteria! Doctor, I love you."

"I love you, too."

She goes off.

7

Mrs. Luztky tells me that one of the patients, Helene, puts worms down her throat and in her bed. I ask her why.

"She's jealous; she never had anything . . . You know she gave gangrene to my cousin Sadie?"

"I thought you didn't like Sadie."

"I love her; she hates me. Dr. Mengele had to sew my eye back in. Agnes sticks wires up my ass. She puts sticks up my vagina. She's a real tiger! She had a hysterectomy. She wants to give me a hysterectomy, too. You should see what they did to my toenail! They cut a hole! They cut my toenail almost in half! They love to kill."

"What do you love to do?"

"I love to help people and make them happy . . . give them a little luxury. You're only on this earth for a short time."

"I thought you could live two million years if you ate sunflower seeds."

"That's only for the birds—they're built stronger. People don't live that long. Maybe a hundred years, if they're lucky."

Another patient, Samantha, comes over. She's telling Mrs. Lutzky about beauty products you can use to keep your skin youthful. Mrs. Lutzky gets very excited.

"Granular scrub? Where do you get that? Revlon? Helena Rubinstein? Any department store? Takes away the dead skin! Takes away the germ, the heptaseptacoccus! Granules! Takes out the poison from the skin!"

Samantha tells her you can get it at the cosmetics counter of any big department store.

"Granules! Takes away the rotten skin! New skin will grow! A real soap opera! Granules! That's a good idea! Better than the benzene! Every department store in America! Takes away the old rotten skin! Then you put tonic on it and it tightens the pores like witch hazel! Your body breaks out, then you have to use witch hazel!"

Samantha: "I want my face to be invigorated and pretty. You get it at Revlon in the department store."

Mrs. Lutzky: "Did you ever put it on your body?"

Samantha: "Yes."

Mrs. Lutzky: "Oh! Granules! . . . my cousin Sadie has rotted skin. I have it too. Mandel comes. He shocks me." Now she turns to me: "I want Sadie to die. . . . I like you. I wish we were married."

"Then what?"

"We'd fight."

"You'd like that."

"Yeah, just like I used to fight with my father and my husband."

8

Mrs. Lutzky is sitting by herself, ordering food out of the air. I sit down next to her. She's getting all kinds of things for breakfast—eggs, bacon, toast, juice, cereal, bananas. She turns to me and tells me that she's ordering food for her son Lennie, and that I look like Lennie. I start ordering food, too, like I'm Lennie: "I want pancakes! With maple syrup . . . Aunt Jemima pancakes with Log Cabin syrup!"

She repeats the order into the air: "An order of pancakes, Aunt Jemima, no, no, make them with Flako pancake batter, that's the best, and Mrs. Butterworth's maple syrup."

This goes on for a while.

Teresa interrupts: "Father, I want the body of Christ. To keep! The Holy Eucharist! It's my life! It's my life!"

Mrs. Lutzky has gotten up. I go into the corridor. She comes up to me.

"You know what's going to happen to me? A lion's going to eat me up!"

"Why would a lion want to eat *you?* Are you that delicious?"

"I don't know . . ."

She seems a little confused.

"A saucer of milk," I say, "that's what they like. They're just big pussycats, anyway."

"You're right. People don't understand that."

"A saucer of milk and a little piece of mouse—a mouseburger, that's what they like!"

"A mouseburger!" she bursts out, then starts laughing. "You're funny!" she says. She's smiling.

Later that afternoon, I go over and tell her that I'm leaving now and will see her next week.

"Goodbye, *mammele*," she says.

"Goodbye, *bubbele*," I reply.

9

Mrs. Lutzky confronts me in the corridor outside the dayroom.

"You don't know what they found under the jetty! They took up the whole New Jersey shore! A pearl as big as a rock!" She goes on and on about the size of these pearls, how much money they're worth. Then she starts talking about Arnie, who was a rock star and a stripper on Forty-Second Street. She tells me what a jerk he was, also Sol Kleinman.

"Sounds like you spent your whole life with a bunch of jerks."

"You said it. . . . I'm not leaving all my money to Sol Kleinman! I want you to go to the Bank of America and take out $150. Go to One Handsome Place, near Wall Street. I want to share it with you. You'll have money and I'll have money; we'll both eat frankfurters together."

"That's a great idea."

She goes off. Then she comes back.

"How much money did I tell you to get? Better make it $300 . . . You think that's enough?"

"It depends on how many frankfurters you want to eat."

She laughs.

"I want pizza, too."

"Better make it $500; that's a good number."

She seems happy.

Outside the building I see her sitting by herself on a bench. I sit down. It's the first time we've ever been outside the building together.

She talks in an entirely different, quite believable way about her family, her early life, and her many hospitalizations. She mentions several other hospitals where she had been institutionalized. She says that she's had many electroshock treatments. She tells me that her mother beat her and that, in the end, her father always sided with her mother against her. This is the first time I have ever heard her speak this way about herself, and I tell her so.

The following week the first thing she wants to know is if I'd gone to the bank for her. I tell her they wouldn't give me the money without her being there, that she'd have to get out of the hospital for us to go to the bank together.

"Are you married?"

"Why do you want to know?"

She proceeds to tell me all the terrible things they do to her and that I have to get her out of here. She goes on to develop an elaborate fantasy of being married to me. No sex, but a lot of shopping and driving around.

10

Mrs. Lutzky tells me that she used to be a race car driver and would drive her family to Elsie's ice cream parlor and buy them banana splits and ice cream sundaes with all kinds of things on top. She says that Adolf Hitler was the greatest man in the world, that there was no one like the Führer. She tells me how the Nazis would torture Jewish women who were giving birth by tying their feet together so they couldn't let the baby out.

"Do you have any idea how much pain that is? Not to be able to let it go?"

I ask her how many children she has. She says seventy-four, and lists the various fathers—Adolf Hitler, Dr. Ting, Dr. Mengele, and so forth. Then she says she's going out for a cigarette and leaves, saying, "I like talking to the doctor."

Coming back into the building, I see her in the vending machines area. She starts talking to me immediately.

"I'm very nervous today. I'm worried about my brother and my father—they're getting stingray bites."

"They went to the beach?"

"Yeah, feeding the snail people in Miami."

We sit down together at a small cafe table. An empty soda can is floating upright on a puddle of water on the tabletop. A fan is blowing and it moves the can around on the puddle.

"Take a look at this," I say to her.

"There's something inside it!"

"What's in there?"

"I don't know!"

"Maybe one of those big black worms that flies. Would you like to see?"

"No! Keep it away from me!"

She gets up and brings me a cup of coffee, then sits down again.

"You're so cute!" she says.

At the end of the day, I approach her in the dayroom to say that I'm leaving and that I will see her next week.

"Only one day a week? How do you make a living if you only come here one day a week?"

"Do you have any better ideas?"

"Why don't you become a pimp? You could send out these women on the ward. Arnie got a Spanish girl in Williamsburg. He gave her Spanish fly and sent her out and she made three hundred dollars a day."

11

"Doctor, I don't feel good. My head hurts. It must have been the hammer. They hit me on the head with a hammer."

"Let me have a look."

She bends over so I can look at the top of her head.

"You're right! You've got a hole this big . . . you must have been hit by something. It's a round hole. I'm not so sure it was a hammer, though. Maybe it was a meatball. It's just about the size of a meatball."

She tells me that they had a picnic yesterday. She had two hamburgers with cheese, two hotdogs with mustard and sauerkraut, a can of soda, two Kool-Aids . . . "What a picnic!" she exclaims, then, "My brother's on his deathbed. My brother's dying . . . My father's dying. I miss my family so." She starts sobbing.

"Why don't you call them to come and visit you?"

"They come here and right away they pull out knives—pen knives. Stab here! Stab there!"

"Who?"

"The patients—they look out the window and watch for them. They see them coming."

"Why don't you do something to stop them?"

"I can't do anything against a hundred men."

"That's true."

"Would you do me a favor?"

"Sure."

"I want you to go to Tiffany's and get me a ring."

"What size?"

She's wearing a small golden ring with a pink rhinestone.

"Here, take this one."

I take the ring, trace the circumference in my notebook, then give it back to her.

"You know what I want? A diamond chip with baguettes all over. Make it about a thousand dollars. Oh, I love you, doctor. I have no mother, no father no more."

It's time to go downstairs to the courtyard for smoking. Mrs. Lutzky gets up and continues talking.

"*Oy!* My head! I got hit with a hammer!"

"A meatball!"

"You know how to make meatballs good? You put green peppers and onion in, then a little soy sauce. Brown them in a pan. Mmmm! Is that good! Just like in the Chinese restaurant . . . Doctor, I think there's something wrong with my brain."

"You want to exchange brains with me?"

"I don't want a man's brain!"

She starts laughing.

"Why not, it might be good for you."

She laughs even louder.

"Me running after women? You're funny, doctor!"

She keeps on laughing.

Teresa comes up: "Father, I want the body of Christ! I want to receive!"

"How do you do that?" I ask her.

"I don't know," she replies, then repeats, "I want to receive."

"I know," I say. She smiles and goes off.

Lucia passes by. "Remember what I told you," she says. "On the wave of consciousness, on the wave of consciousness."

Mrs. Lutzky continues. "I want you to take out my counterfeit money. Uncle Moe's got it on Hackett Street. We'll go shopping at Gucci. We'll go to the Blarney Stone and see someone do a striptease." She points to Agnes, who's sitting across the room.

"She's dangerous, that Agnes. She put a wire up my heinie! She had a hysterectomy, so she wants me to have it, too. She's jealous."

Lucia comes and quietly sits down next to me. After a while, I hand her the notebook and pen, still maintaining my conversation with Mrs. Lutzky. She writes: "To Doctor Poser, I love you so much as my pediatrician (my baby doctor) and psychiatrist. Love always, Lucia Alighieri." She hands it back and I take it silently. Teresa is now mimicking Mrs. Lutzky but stops to ask me again for the body of Christ. Mrs. Lutzky asks if I will protect her in the hospital if she pays me. She asks me to bring her some Johnson and Johnson's baby shampoo when I come back next week.

"It's a blackboard jungle in here," she says.

12

The night before going to the hospital, I have a dream about Mrs. Lutzky. She's died and I've been called before the hospital administrators to account for it. I can't explain how it happened—I don't know how or why, but it's not my fault. The whole thing has the atmosphere of an inquisition. Then I'm in the ward and she's standing in line waiting to go out for smoking. I feel like I've been duped, that she's made a fool out of me.

The next morning, coming down the corridor in the ward, I pass by a private room with the door open. Mrs. Lutzky's in a hospital bed with a sling around her neck. I go in.

"What's up?"

"I broke my collar bone. You remember I was telling you my bed kept moving on me? Well, last night I put the pillow in the middle of the bed to try to get comfortable and all of a sudden, Boom! I was on the floor! I'll be all right. Red China will grow me a new collar bone. They didn't want to operate."

I tell her I have to go on into the dayroom now, but I'll be back.

"You'll come back?"

"I'll come back and see you."

"In a little while? Please come back. I missed you."

"I missed you, too, I'll be back later."

13

Mrs. Lutzky comes and sits next to me. She's complaining about her Uncle Moe.

"Everybody should be a mouse except him!" She tells me she wants me to go to Tiffany's and buy her a diamond pinky ring for about $2,500. She asks me if I know what size, and, as we have done before, I trace the circumference of her rhinestone ring in my notebook.

"I feel bad for him," she says, "but he doesn't feel bad for me . . . the money went to his head . . ." She turns her head away and starts talking into the air: "Little Italy? You hear me? Pizza store? I want fifteen pizzas for the girls this time. By five o'clock? Eighty-five dollars? Thanks a lot. Bill it to the Rifkin Bank—they take care of everything."

She looks over at me writing.

"That's some kind of shorthand. I learned shorthand once."

I ask her to show me. She writes some symbols down but doesn't seem to know what they mean.

"So young, I had everything to live for and they rolled me down a hill."

Teresa comes over: "Father, I want the body of Christ and the Holy Eucharist."

"What for?"

"I want to keep it in my holy sacrament case."

Helene shrieks at her from a short distance away:

"Don't point at me! She stuck her finger in my vagina, you dirty bitch!"

Teresa becomes very agitated. She repeats over and over, ". . . past, present, and future; past, present, and future . . ."

Mrs. Lutzky continues talking into the air:

"The German Army burned me with flamethrowers! I sent you. Why did you go in there again? You . . . the world's full of mean bastards! Mother Cabrini's killing off the white people, taking the sinew. And my brother Morris's sinew. They're cooking it and feeding it to the pigs! There's a better diet for pigs than the sinew of people! You just don't like white people!"

Now she's talking to me again: "They'll throw you out the window!"

"They'll make scrambled eggs out of you," I say. "We'll have to scrape you off the sidewalk with a spatula."

"How do I love thee? Let me count the ways."

"That sounds like a poem."

"I wrote poems and sonnets. I wrote cookbooks, too. I had my own cookbook store. I used to dance the Hoochie Coochie at the Blarney Stone."

"A regular Gypsy Rose Lee."

"I used to shake my fanny at the Blarney Stone."

"Can you still do it? Let's see you do it now."

"You're so cute! I'd like to choke you!"

"That would feel good."

"Moe was such a mean bastard, no different than me. He's loaded. He loves my cousin Sadie, he hates me. He chops off my head."

"He'd love to see you die."

"I do all the work, she waits . . . I want to get you a diamond necklace with a diamond ring for your wife."

Now she's talking into the air:

"Tiffany's? I'm sending Doctor Poser to get a diamond necklace and a ring—the ring should be about six thousand dollars."

"What would you like me to get you, a parachute? Then when they throw you out the window, you won't splatter!"

She laughs. I feel like I'm trading lines with her in a Jewish comedy routine and that it's doing both of us a lot of good.

"It gives me *naches* when I buy you something," she says. "You'll have nice things . . . You know Sharon Tate? She had a body you wouldn't believe! She was married to a doctor. I want you to get a counterfeiting machine in Brooklyn."

"What if I get caught? They'll put me in jail and I couldn't come here to see you anymore."

"I'll get you off, if the cops get you . . . Nah, you better not do it . . . Better you make an honest living . . . I wish we could be counterfeiters together. Ooh, I'd like that! I'd like that! . . . Doctor, I'm afraid I'm going through a lion's den. I was a mischievous kid, riding on peoples' backs. Piggyback riding. Did I ever tell you I rode a Brahma bull elephant? He gave me a ride on his back. I gave him a lollypop, something to eat, a little piece of sandwich, I think."

"No wonder he gave you ride on his back."

"Doctor, I want a grilled cheese sandwich . . . I'm worried about them in Red China. I'm worried about them in Germany, too. The Führer in the modern world . . . You'll live like a king, if you don't start another war. You want everything for yourself! Boy oh boy! I've seen everything! Nice people you want to kill!"

"Like you."

"Nice people like you . . . Uncle Moe made shit out of me, everything is Sadie, . . . I love my mother."

"You love your mother."

"No, you don't need a mother. The milk supply is in your body. No, you don't need a mother."

14

"Hi, Doctor, did you hear about the bugs they've got in New York now? Giant bugs, like water bugs, I think. They're all over the place!"

"Do they bite?"

"They ate the eyes right out of my brother's head! He has no skin anymore!"

"Can you kill them?"

"I think they're afraid of matches . . . How are you?"

"I'm fine."

"How come you never wear the watch I gave you?"

"I'm afraid someone will steal it."

"You'll get mugged!"

"I'll get mugged by one of the *meshuggenahs* in here!"

She breaks out laughing.

Teresa comes up to me. "Father, I want to tell you something. I want the body of Christ and the Holy Eucharist, but when I get it, I want to keep it."

"You want to keep it . . . forever and ever."

"Yes," she says, breaking into a broad grin, "forever and ever."

Bob Dylan is singing on the radio: "*How does it feel? How does it feel? To be on your own, with no direction home, like a complete unknown, like a rolling stone?*" Some patients get up and start dancing and singing along with the music. Now it's the Jefferson Airplane:

"Don't you want somebody to love? Don't you need somebody to love? Wouldn't you love somebody to love?"

Mrs. Lutzky asks me to come downstairs and have a cup of coffee, she'll buy me one. We go downstairs together. She tells me she can't eat the food they serve her in the hospital, that they gave her a veal cutlet that was made of all breadcrumbs, no meat, that the chef who cooks for the food service is a wise guy.

"Come on," she says, "I want to buy you something."

"Buy for yourself."

"What's wrong with you?"

"What's wrong with *you?*"

I go and buy myself a cup of coffee.

"I'll buy a roll," she says, "we'll share it."

She buys the roll and then goes and gets herself a soda. We sit down.

"Doctor Poser, I'm sorry I said, 'What's wrong with you?'"

"What are you sorry for? Maybe there *is* something wrong with me."

"There's something wrong with *me!*"

"There's something wrong with everybody."

"Yeah," she says, laughing.

We share the roll. She goes to buy a Mounds bar and loses her money in the machine. We go to the desk attendant nearby to report it. I give her the change to buy another Mounds bar. She offers me half. I decline and tell her I'll see her later, then leave the building.

15

I meet Mrs. Lutzky by the vending machines.

"I wish you would marry me," she exclaims.

"Huh?"

"I wish you would marry me."

"That's what I thought you said."

She says that Isabel put a hundred rats down her throat, that she poisoned Arnie's water. She says she's not going to eat the food they serve her upstairs, that she's only going to eat from the vending machines. She tells me she wishes they sold egg rolls in the vending machines, that if they had egg rolls in the vending machines you could heat them up in the microwave and they would come with a little package of duck sauce and you could make a fortune if you could sell egg rolls here like that. I agree that it would be a great idea. She says her cousin Sadie has the streptococcus virus and the tsetse fly disease, that she's a patient at St. Luke's.

"Did you know that New York has the highest percentage of paranoia in the country, paranoid schizophrenia?"

"Is that what you have?"

"That's what they wrote on my chart, that I had hallucinations . . . they feed me scraps like for a dog—Gravy Train dog food they feed me."

I go on out of the building for a break.

Back upstairs on the ward, Mrs. Lutzky is causing a commotion on account of refusing to take her medication, which she is given by injection. She won't budge.

"It's Moe's idea!" she's yelling. "He won't even miss me! I'm going to die!"

Several therapy aides are trying to reassure her that she won't die, that she has to get up and come down the hall to get her shot.

"She's refusing to take her medications," says Lucia. "She's afraid she's going to die . . . Is that the worst that can happen?"

"Is it?"

"I don't know," she replies.

I get up, go straight over to Mrs. Lutzky and tell her that now it's time for us to chop her head off and that once she's dead she can have egg rolls in Heaven, that she can have all the egg rolls in Heaven that she wants. She laughs, gets up, and goes with the therapy aides down the hall. She returns in a few minutes, quite calm and cheerful.

"How'd you like a pink face," she says, "a nice tint? That would look very good on you!"

"I'll bet it would!" I reply.

16

Three days before Christmas.

Agnes is curled up in her chair by the door into the dayroom as I come in. She opens her eyes.

"Hi," I say. "How are you?"

She closes her eyes again.

I go sit with Mrs. Lutzky. She tells me they chopped up her mother and made hamburger and sausage out of her. She wants me to go to Tiffany's and buy her a diamond heart for a hundred dollars, diamond earrings for about two thousand, and bring back some egg rolls. ". . . five egg rolls—three for you and two for me. Also, spring rolls, a bucket of spareribs—a big bucket of spareribs."

"What else do you want?"

"I'd like a new dress, a cheap dress for about twenty dollars, black. Also, a box of candy, chocolate, Whitman's Sampler, a box of cordial cherries. Buy something for yourself, too. Up to ten thousand dollars. Go to the Rifkin Bank of New Jersey."

She starts talking into the air: "Rifkin Bank? I'm sending someone to the bank for me to take out about ten thousand dollars . . . Egg rolls for everybody, lots of duck sauce, lo mein, lobster Cantonese, ten buckets, ten buckets of Chinese spare ribs, sweet and sour pork, ten buckets, sweet and sour chicken, ten buckets, shrimp chow mein, ten buckets, you better bring it in a grocery wagon, fortune cookies, pistachio ice cream, pepper steak, we're having a Chinese party, pork fried rice, ice cream, butter pecan, paper plates, spoons . . ."

She pauses and looks over at Agnes asleep in the chair.

"Agnes is sleeping. She's afraid of something. She touched my cousin with the streptococcus. She's all nerved up."

Teresa comes over and asks me for the body of Christ.

Across the room, Lily bursts out in an angry voice with a Southern accent: "I don't want you in my house! I don't want you! I'm getting rid of all of you someday because I hate all of you! You never let me have one moment of peace! You never let me have one day without you! I can't stand you!"

Mrs. Lutzky continues. She says she had a picture of her breasts published in *Playboy*.

"Arnie said I had the most beautiful breasts he'd ever seen. I won the *Playboy* contest . . . I had thirty-four children . . . I gave them all Chocolate Kisses. I bought up the Hershey's chocolate factory."

Agnes gets up from her chair and comes over.

"Merry Christmas," she says. "How are you? I'm waking up, just waking up. I've got to go now."

Mrs. Lutzky calls out to Isabel: "I love you! You're beautiful! You could be a model, Isabel! Me, I look like E.T.!"

Isabel stares at her and says, "I'm afraid."

"You have tears!" says Mrs. Lutzky. "Now stop it!"

Isabel goes off.

Agnes is holding herself and rocking.

Mrs. Lutzky is quiet for a moment, then continues: "Paranoia's only a form of getting hurt by something. When you're paranoid, you're afraid of getting hurt by something. I don't think I'm paranoid. Voodoo they did on me at these hospitals. Demons coming out of my mouth. I'm lucky to be alive. They told me I had yellow jaundice in Red China. . . . I can't take stress. I remember my first nervous breakdown. My mother and my husband were having a fight in the house. I was cooking at the stove. My hands started shaking, I was broiling fish at the stove. My hand started going like this"—she shakes her hand in a rapid tremor—" 'I feel sick,' I said, 'You better take me to the hospital' . . . When you have schizophrenia, you can't take much stress. They should give you money. Then you can come here, talk to people, get paid . . . They think they own you! They should stick it in their beard!"

17

Mrs. Lutzky confronts me as soon as I come into the dayroom. She says there's been a car accident—her brother Morris and her little boy, Baby Lennie, were killed. They were driving in traffic. Another patient is standing nearby, laughing ridiculously. Mrs. Lutzky notices her.

"She's laughing!" Mrs. Lutzky exclaims, then turns to her and screams: "I'll bang your head against the wall and you'll be dead!"

Then she turns back to me: "I gotta get out of here, already! I never hear any good news!" Then she starts crying.

"My baby! I don't want to live any more if my children are dead! I miss my husband and my children. You know what Arnie says? The best way to kill someone is to marry them first. He doesn't love me. He wants to knife me. He just got married again. He doesn't give a shit!

"I'm vomiting all my food and he wants me to go to the bank to get money!"

We sit down together on a couch. She turns her back to me and curls up. She starts talking into the air: ". . . chocolate cake, fresh from Shop-Rite . . . my kids are gonna die and I'm gonna live? No way! It's not gonna happen!"

"You're a tough bird to kill."

"I'm not that tough."

"You're vulnerable."

18

"I'm going to give you five hundred dollars and I want you to call the Bronx Zoo. They've got my brother, my father, and Baby Lennie locked up in a cage and they're going to feed them to the lions! Please, do it! Promise me! I'll call the Bank of New York to send you a check."

"I want the money first," I say. "How do I know you're not going to cheat me?"

"Call the zoo! Please! I'm afraid they'll put them in with the lions."

"I'll see what I can do about it."

She goes off. I go to the other side of the room to sit with Agnes. Mrs. Lutzky follows in a few minutes. "They're home! They're OK. I want you to have the five hundred dollars anyway."

Then she looks at me, smiling very girlishly. "I think I'm in love with you."

"You've got some taste in men!" I say. "Look, I think I'm losing my hair!"

"Put some Abilene cream and dog shit on your head; it'll grow back . . . coal tar, that's good, too, but it makes your skin turn black. I was some doctor, you know. I did brain surgery. You got a tumor growing in your head you gotta cut it right off, right at the roots, like a sweet potato. Rip it right out of the head! Then you put the Tootsie lollypop in the head, so it won't grow back. I think I've got blood poisoning—all that stuff they put into me—worm juice, killer ants . . ."

"I think I've got blood poisoning, too," I tell her.

"You? How did *you* get blood poisoning?"

"I eat here. I breathe here. I go to the bathroom. It's all over the place."

"Did you know that my father put a picture of my tits in *Playboy*? They said I had the most beautiful breasts in the world. Arnie's killing my father. They're burning my mother in the oven. They rattle her bones so she can't even go to sleep to die."

All of a sudden, I get extremely tired, like I'm going to keel over right there and then. I tell her I'll be right back, then leave the day-room to sit by myself in the staff break room.

19

Mrs. Lutzky is in the vending machines area eating a roll with butter. She asks me if I want a soda. She says the nurse is touching her with her red hands, that the nurse's hands are red from touching Sol Kleinman.

"I figured out what they're trying to do to me—give me jungle rot! They're throwing dirty water on me! Then they pour on soap suds."

A patient comes up to her asking for money. She gives him a dollar.

"You're a very generous person," I say.

She starts ordering food out of the air: "Send half of the Key Food to Dachau today! Bananas with sour cream, fish sticks with tartar sauce—the fish sticks are still good—a hundred of them, frozen chicken, pound cake, garlic and onions, anisette cookies, ice cream and cake, rolls, buttered rolls, crullers, donuts—all kinds of donuts, stuffed cabbage, hamburger, chopped meat, bacon, American cheese, frankfurters, relish—55 bottles of relish, 10 cases of soda—Coca Cola, Pepsi Cola, Mountain Dew, big Hershey chocolate bars—the black chocolate, chocolate cake. All right, that's enough for now. To Dachau today! They gotta eat! Survival of the fittest! You bite me, I'll bite you back!"

"There you go," I say.

"Someone put an old razor on my face. Arnie, go put moisturizer on your face. . . . I could tell you stories for hours how they treated me and my cousin. They're jealous! They put an old razor on my face! They're going to scrape off the skin! What should I do?"

"What about getting a Doberman pinscher?"

"He'll lick my face! . . . You're crazy, doctor! . . . I'm all bloody! They poisoned me!"

"I nearly passed out in here last week!" I say.

"Did you hit your head?"

"No, I'm OK."

"Watch who comes in your house . . . Do you think they're coming after you because you're hanging around with me?"

"Sounds right . . . We're in it together. We're in the soup together."

20

Mrs. Lutzky tells me she went to the dentist and he took out all her teeth, cut up her tongue, and sewed up her gums. "Now he wants money! I'll give him money! I'll give him a brain tumor!"

"Madame, can I take your order now? Would you like to start with something from the bar?"

She brightens up immediately. "I'll have a whiskey sour."

"Appetizer?"

"I'll have antipasto."

"And for an entrée?"

"Eggplant parmesan and baked ziti."

"Some vegetables to go with that? You can have peas, carrots, spinach, escarole . . ."

"I'll have carrots. I'd like some chicken soup, noodle soup with pieces of chicken. And give me some cut-up red potatoes with dressing, cooked in the oven . . . You make me laugh." She switches into a TV cowboy accent: "I'm gonna git you, you varmint, you!"

Lucia is dancing to the music videos on the television, spins around a few times, and goes back to her chair.

"Now for dessert."

"Fruit cocktail, peaches and pears, with some sherbet . . . I've got a heart problem. I've got a hole in my heart."

"That's a problem."

"I got a hole in my head, too."

"Getting hit with too many meatballs."

She smiles.

"You know what takes away athlete's foot? Rose lotion. Takes away jungle rot, too."

Isabel is sitting nearby watching the music videos on the TV. All of a sudden she exclaims: "Between two women! To do *that* to one another—I never saw that before! . . . I like men!"

Teresa pipes up: "I like the body of Christ, you know."

Mrs. Lutzky has gone off to stand by the windows, staring out into space.

21

Mrs. Lutzky sits down and starts talking about a television character she likes—Miss Piggy—and how the actress who plays Miss Piggy has to be all made up to look like that.

"Not much," I tell her, "she really looks like that, they don't really have to make her up very much at all. Did you know that that woman lives in a big co-op on Central Park West and gets driven to the television studio in a limousine every day to do the show?"

"Oh, come on, Doctor, I don't believe that! You must be putting me on!"

I just look at her.

She starts laughing, then says, "I think you're crazy!"

22

I sit down next to Mrs. Lutzky. She starts complaining about Isabel.

"I'll fix your ass! Cut his throat! The sergeant sees what's going on! They took my brother to Melrose hospital! They took out bone marrow!"

She talks about Geritol and estrogen. "I had a lot of children. I need hormones, vitamins. I need estrogen. I'm all *farkakteh!*"

She tells me she'd like to own the dog races in Florida, that she already owns Hialeah and the jai alai stadium. She says she needs to feed her children macaroni and cheese with a little tomato sauce.

"Babies like that. I've seen it on TV, little elbow macaronis."

I ask her if she knows how to make pasta.

"I gotta turn over and go to sleep."

"Fine, go to sleep."

Lucia is asleep in a chair in the rear of the dayroom. I go over and sit down next to her. She wakes up, dazed.

"Hi, Doctor Poser," she says. "I was dreaming of you."

She coughs.

"I don't feel well," she says.

"A touch of the flu seems to be going around . . . What was the dream?"

"You were trying to talk to me, but I was rude."

"You don't have to talk if you don't feel like it."

"OK," she says, and goes back to sleep.

Mrs. Lutzky is sitting up in her chair. I go back to sit with her.

"They cut off my legs at the hip."

"But you've still got them."

"They're just stuck on," she says.

"Can you wiggle your toes?"

"Yes."

"That's an illusion. When they cut off your legs, they sever the nerves. You think you can feel your toes, but it's only your imagination."

"I can wiggle them a little . . . I want Chinese food. How much is three or four dozen egg rolls?"

"I'm making a party here in May. I'm getting pizza for everybody else, but maybe I'll get some Chinese food for you."

"You better not, they'll get jealous. Just get pizza."

23

Coming out of the building, I meet the rabbi affiliated with the hospital. We've met before. He greets me and asks me to remind him of my name. I tell him my name. I ask him if he's going to do anything for Purim with the patients. He says he's got a box of *hamantaschen* in the trunk of his car and he's planning to give them to the patients at his regular Jewish services. He says that there's a patient he knows I talk to, Mrs. Lutzky, and that he would like to talk to me about her some time. I suggest we talk right now. He asks me to walk him to his car. He says he's known Mrs. Lutzky for many years, that all he ever gets from her are terrible delusions of torture and mutilation. He says she seems to experience him as two different people, sometimes one and sometimes the other, and that a psychologist at her former hospital told him that she did something called "object-splitting." I tell him I have never been able to get her to relinquish her delusions, but that she's very interested in food and recipes, that she could recite the entire menu of a Jewish delicatessen, and that he might find that she would respond to an invitation to help him plan the menu for a party or celebratory meal. He thanks me for this suggestion, then gets into his car.

Back upstairs on the ward, I mention to Mrs. Lutzky that I had just spoken to the rabbi and that he was going to be giving out *hamantaschen* at a Purim party.

"That bastard tried to convert me to Christianity!" she bursts out. "The *hamantaschen* are poisoned!"

"Oh, boy! I really got taken in! Thank you for telling me!"

"I've got oil under the skin."

"Then how come you're so dry and flaky?"

"I got too much *tsouris!* I bring back the dead."

"You can grow new hair too, isn't that so?"

"Abilene cream and dog shit, just put it on your head."

"We tried that already. I'm your first failure."

24

"I'm too skinny-looking. I'm losing all this weight because I can't eat the food here."

"A human skeleton, just like in Auschwitz."

"They're eating mice over there . . . I've got to send them some nice food to eat—roast chicken and potatoes, peas and carrots, meatballs and spaghetti with tomato sauce . . . They're trying to poison me here! They give me mice to eat; I'm getting food poisoning!"

"Did you know that if you sauté the mice in mothballs, that takes out all the bad germs?"

"Really? I never heard of that!"

"I'm serious, it really works. Another thing you can do is marinate them in milk of magnesia before you cook them."

She looks at me incredulously.

"I'm going to hit you over the head with a hammer!"

I look alarmed.

"I scared you!" she says, quite pleased with herself.

I give her a big smile.

"Yes, you certainly did."

25

Mrs. Lutzky says she wants to come to live with me and my wife, and that she'd clean the house and wash the Venetian blinds every six months.

"I'll get a Jewish cookbook and make kugel."

"Can you roast a chicken?"

"Of course I can roast a chicken! I'll make you rich, I'll work hard. I'll go scuba diving under the ocean to find diamonds."

"What about making a show? You could sing a few Barbra Streisand songs and do a belly dance."

"Moe is up to no good. He doesn't love me. He loves Sadie. You know what he said? I'm shit, Sadie's a queen."

She looks over at me writing in my notebook.

"You look like you're writing Chinese."

"I'm practicing."

"How'd you learn to write Chinese? You're so clever, Doctor, I'd like to buy you a diamond ring."

"I'll write, you order."

"I'll have two egg rolls, shrimp sweet and sour, lobster lo mein."

I write her name in two vertical columns of script and show it to her.

"It's Chinese!"

She continues recounting her woes: "Sadie takes off all her clothes and gets on top of me; she wants to give me her disease. Agnes sticks wires up my ass. She sticks knives up there and makes me bleed!"

She tells me about a store in Far Rockaway where you can buy a dress for fifty cents. "Who wants to wear a *shmatte* like that? Looks like a rag from the Salvation Army! Every day of my life I'm wearing *shmattes,* old lady dresses . . . it's amazing how you write Chinese."

"I gotta keep practicing."

"Oh, I miss my father . . . seventeen years . . . someone threw him down the stairs . . . my mother was a good woman. So she liked to fool around . . . I like to fool around, too."

She's gone to the wardrobe shop downstairs and comes back wearing a bright purple sweater and pink pants. I tell her how nice she looks in her new clothes. She says that they're too big, she wants smaller sizes. She gets up and asks the nurse if they can get her clothes in smaller sizes. She comes back.

"I haven't got long to live. I'm an old lady. I've got a heart murmur."

I start singing "Sam, You Made the Pants Too Long."

She starts laughing, then says, "Oh, Doctor, you're so smart! *Oy!* . . . I was fine when I was a kid. Like a *shtick holz!* Then Dr. Mandel got a hold of me and gave me shock treatments."

"They fixed you but good."

"Arnie wants my money. He tells me he loves me, he misses me, but all he wants is my money. . . . I was married to Hitler. We used to drink beer and smoke cigarettes. You should'a seen him ice skate! He could ice skate better than Sonja Henie! Me, too! . . . I've got amnesia for all those years. They shocked me . . . You're writing a love story."

She becomes quiet, reflective.

I just sit there.

26

"So how are you, Doctor?"

"How are you?"

"I got pains. My leg bothers me."

"The one they amputated?"

She laughs.

"They'll have to give me curettage . . . I'm not going to the Passover seder, you don't know that rabbi. He's not working for me; he's working for Moe. He's taking money out of my wallet."

"So tell me, why is this night different from all other nights?"

"You want a punch? You're a real card!"

Teresa starts badgering me for the body of Christ.

"You see this one?" I say to Mrs. Lutzky. "She's a real *nudnik*."

"She's a *nudnik* and I'm a *kvetch*," she replies.

A social worker comes over to ask Mrs. Lutzky if she's going to the Passover seder. Mrs. Lutzky says she's not only Jewish but Inca, that she loves her Jewish mother and her Jewish father, but she doesn't get along with the rabbi, that he calls her a *shmatte*. The social worker leaves. Mrs. Lutzky then continues talking to me: "You know what they're doing in Florida? Feeding the sharks at the hotels. They come right up to the beach."

"What do they feed them?"

"Big chunks of meat . . . horse meat, I think."

Claire has come over and is lying on a couch with her head toward me. "Punish her for her illness," she mutters.

Mrs. Lutzky asks me whether I want to go out with her after lunch to have a bagel and cream cheese at the vending machines.

At this point, Joanna staggers into the side of a chair, starts to topple, and is helped into the chair by another patient. She's watching something invisible on the ceiling. She gets up and starts following it, her eyes turned up in her head. Lucia gets up, intercepts her, and puts her in another chair. She comes back. "Doctor Poser," she says, "you see Joanna? She's having a seizure."

Mrs. Lutzky is ordering food, a hotdog a million miles long and pizza from the Pizza Hut. ". . . ambrosia, all kinds of fruit, apples, peaches, all kinds of coconuts and sour cream . . ."

Joanna is beating her arms on the sides of her chair.

Mrs. Lutzky is talking about tongue: ". . . Let my grandfather get a bunch of tongues and send them up in Italian bread with mustard . . . Boy, is that good! Cow's tongue, with a big chunk of onion and frankfurters with relish, spinach and potatoes with chicken . . . John Travolta took two thousand dollars from me for pizza and it never came . . ."

In the afternoon, the social worker comes back to the ward. She's got a paper plate with two matzohs for Mrs. Lutzky. Everybody wants some. She breaks off little pieces for all the patients in the ward. She offers me some.

"What is it?" I ask.

"Matzoh; you don't know what matzoh is?"

"Tell me."

"That's when Moses took the Jews out of Egypt and parted Red Sea. They ate unleavened bread . . . the parting of the Red Sea."

I take a little piece and we eat together.

27

The room becomes chaotic. Everyone starts yelling, crying, or singing.

Helene is screaming at the nurse: "These drugs are for children! I've got a Ph.D. in Pharmacology! I want to be with girls because I'm a girl!"

Another patient is pacing around muttering, "What good is it? What good is it?" over and over.

I go sit with Mrs. Lutzky.

"I've got two weeks to live!" she says.

"Then you'll miss the party . . . well, if I don't see you again, it was nice knowing you."

"*Oy, mamenyu! Kayne horeh!*"

She starts laughing, then leans over closer to me.

"You wanna hear about the kinky sex I had with Rocco? I wouldn't take it in the mouth, so I tied it up with a string and hit it with a hammer!"

She seems very pleased with herself. She asks me if I have change of a dollar. I ask her if she has change of a hundred dollar bill. She says she's worried about her children, Harriet and Lennie, that Sol Kleinman's locked them in a closet and they can't shit.

"*Oy, Gotenyu!*" I exclaim.

"You know how many children I've got? Sixty-four children! I can't take care of Lily Marlene! . . . My Red China, the sleeping giant of the world. You know what my Uncle Moe would say about you? A real humdinger!"

"A real humdinger."

"I used to call up doctors all the time—skin doctors. You shoulda seen the phone bills! Fifty-dollar phone bills!"

"That's a lot!"

"I was burned! Arnie walked out on me . . . they put me in the psych ward."

She falls silent.

Later that afternoon, I go downstairs to the vending machines. Mrs. Lutzky finds me there. She buys ice cream and potato chips. She sits down next to me.

"You ever play mahjong?" I ask her.

"No, but canasta, what a game *that* is! . . . I miss my mother . . . Oh my God. No one screamed louder than my mother."

28

Mrs. Lutzky is at the vending machines. She buys cheese and crackers for herself and also something for another patient on the ward.

"Doctor Poser, take me to the Bank of New York. I'll give you a hundred dollars . . . Do you really have to leave?"

"You want me to stay?"

"I'll tell you what you should do. Accept Medicaid. Then people will come. You'll have plenty of money. . . . Sol Kleinman divorced me. You wanna hear about the kinky sex I had with Arnie? I got on top of him and made like a man."

"You showed him a thing or two."

"Isabel puts glass down my throat, broken pieces of china . . . Doctor, I'm so unhappy! Why are they always picking on me? I'm a scapegoat! I'm too fancy! I'm a fancy one!"

She smiles.

"Do you have to leave? Why don't you do what Mandel did—he charges everybody the same, sixty-five dollars a visit and he takes Medicare . . . Let's get married!"

"You like that idea."

"I love you!"

29

Mrs. Lutzky's hair is wet, as though she just got out of the shower.

"How are you? You look spiffy, all cleaned up."

"I stink! I've got body odor down there! I think men are coming into my room and climbing on top of me at night! I'm full of come down there! I need a douche! About a thousand of them jumping on me! They're making a cesspool out of me! I need to be douched out!"

"That's a very pretty blouse you've got on. What color is it?"

"Hot pink—the rosebud color, a kind of fuchsia—that's the latest color . . . and blonde hair, very light, what they used to call 'platinum blonde.' They wash my hair in dirty water here. Moe doesn't want me to have no more petty cash. They'll give out the petty cash while I'm sleeping. He's drinking champagne and I can't even have ten dollars?"

"Who, Moe?"

"Yeah, stingiest man I ever seen . . . I'm only forty-seven! He's got a casket for me in his house already!"

"He's a monster."

"They threw my father down the stairs when I was seventeen years old. They want to take me out of here and throw me in the East River to the sharks. . . . Anything that happens to me, happens to them! Anything that happens to me, happens to them! . . . I don't know how I'm alive! Arnie's throwing bugs down my throat! Threw my mother out the window four times!"

She gets up to go the bathroom.

When she comes out, the TV is showing a picture of Bernhard Goetz, the man who shot several Black teenagers on the subway and is being sued for fifty million dollars. She starts talking to him:

"You'll get yours, Bernhard Goetz! You're gonna threaten me and my cousin? You'll die yourself! Who the hell do you think you are? You're a gangster! You're threatening me and Moe, Sadie and every-body? I'll threaten *you!* Who the hell do you think you are? We won't live good any more? Let him go to hell, Machine! He's got big eyes on the family!"

30

This is my last regular day on the ward before the going-away party I'm throwing next week. Mrs. Lutzky greets me when I come into the dayroom.

"How are you?" I ask her.

"Not too well."

"What's bothering you?"

"These girls, they don't know when to stop! They're killing me! Drawing a line in the sky. They're jealous. They think they're going to get rid of me and my whole family and take all my money, live it up!"

"Fat chance."

"They're all going to die! There's going to be a big funeral! You don't know what they did to my mother in Melrose State! They had a big saw coming down from the ceiling! Sawed off her arms and legs! They had a big piece of glass, hot! Hotter than cremation! They put it right on her!"

I get called away to the phone. I come back to Mrs. Lutzky. She looks sad.

"You look sad."

"I am; they're going to cut my legs off. . . . What a life I coulda had. I was a great doctor for ten years."

"That's a long time."

"Boy, was I making money! Fifty thousand dollars a week!"

She gets up to get her petty cash. She gets it, sits down, and starts talking into the air: "You took my money away from me 'cause you don't want me to be happy! Everything for you, Moe! I hope you die already! Die already! You're the meanest guy I ever seen in my life! You robbed me of four dollars!"

A nurse comes in and tells her it's time for her medication shot. She goes off and comes back in a few minutes.

"Doctor Pagel, I don't want to live no more! They give me lithium and arsenic right in the hip bone! They want to cripple me! Right in the hip bone! They want to cripple me! . . . It's a pity. They're making a piece of shit out of me! What a waste! . . . Oh, Doctor, what am I going to do?"

"You better stay in a safe place."

"There *is* no safe place! They tried to come in here last night and kidnap me, take me out of here in a wheelchair!"

31

My last day at the hospital. We're outside in the grassy courtyard, with picnic tables and a gazebo. The party is nearly over. I've already said goodbye to most of the other patients. I go over to Mrs. Lutzky, who's sitting on a bench, still eating. She says the pizza was good, that she's eaten so much she has to get the last piece in with a shoehorn.

"You're going to miss us already," she says.

"I always will."

"Why are you leaving? To make more money, right? It's better you get out of here anyway."

"What about you?"

"I'm dead meat! I got an infection in my ear, the German army killed my mother, broke her bones, one at a time! They put her in the oven!"

"What do you want from me?"

She smiles.

"A kiss on the cheek."

I give it to her.

She turns and goes off toward the building.

PART III
Lucia

1

First impression. Lucia is relentlessly plodding up and down the long corridor that connects the heavy metal entry door to the ward and the dayroom at the far end. She's drooling and continuously shaking her left hand from the wrist, her dark hair stuck to her face with perspiration. She speaks continuously, sometimes to herself, sometimes to someone who isn't there:

". . . fifty days and fifty days . . . another hundred days . . . fifty days and fifty days . . . another hundred days . . . fifty days and fifty days . . . another hundred days . . ." Her voice shifts to anger: "What do you mean, there's a war going on? No one told you to die when I yelled at you! How chicken can you be?" Her voice shifts again to sweet soothing, like a mother comforting a child: "There, there, honey; it's all right . . . There, there, little girl . . ." She keeps repeating these phrases over and over as she paces up and down the corridor several times. She makes eye contact with no one. Each time she passes me, I face toward her. Each time, she walks right past me with no sign of recognition that I'm even there. I make no effort to contact her.

2

The dayroom is completely chaotic. Everyone is laughing, screaming, talking out loud, or moving around. The nurse is coming to give a class on mental and physical health. Lucia is making scanning movements with her hands held up in front of her face, as though she were looking through binoculars. When she scans me, she says, "I know you. You're the professor from Heidelberg. You're Professor Heidelberg." She seems very pleased to recognize me.

The nurse goes to the center of the room.

"Okay ladies. Let's settle down. We're going to have a little class on mental and physical health. Now I want each of you to tell me what your diagnosis is and what medication you are taking. Agnes, would you like to begin?"

Agnes (sounding like a nursery school child): "I need a witness to tell me what I'm doing. I'm wounded."

Nurse: "Well, that may be true, but it's not a diagnosis. . . . How can a doctor treat you when he doesn't know what he's treating?"

Agnes: "I know what's wrong with me: I've got brain damage! My IQ is too high!"

Nicole (dreamily): "I take two medications: one's for rats, one's for mice."

Agnes is now rocking back and forth with nonstop talk, no longer engaged with the nurse or anyone else in the room.

Lucia (to the nurse): "I used to be at Saint Elizabeth's. I liked it there. I don't like it here so much. I had a nervous breakdown. All my love turned into hate."

Nurse (looking around): "Okay. Enough of that. Now we're going to talk about food."

Several patients express their approval.

Nurse: "Good. Now there are five kinds of food that we all should eat to stay healthy. Does anyone know what they are?"

The patients start drifting off, not paying very much attention, going back to original chaos.

Nurse: "Well, there's fruit, vegetables, cereals, meats, and dairy."

Lucia begins singing: "*I'm Chiquita Banana, and I've come to say / Bananas have to ripen in a certain way / When they are flecked with brown and have a golden hue / Bananas taste the best and they're the best for you . . .*" She stops singing and is now speaking directly to the nurse: "Agnes doesn't have brain damage. She's a baby. I gave birth to her this morning. I've got the birth certificate to prove it." She turns toward me and addresses me directly: "I've got seventeen children. I've got lots of uncles and aunts and cousins. She's the one; I'm not the one. Lucia. Lucia Alighieri. Miss Alighieri."

Nurse: "Lucia, can you tell me whether a tomato is a fruit or a vegetable?"

Lucia: "I think it's a fruit."

The nurse compliments her on giving the right answer, then introduces me by name to the group.

Lucia to me: "Dr. Poser, I'm not making fun of you, but I think we're blood-related."

I give her a warm smile. She gives me two thumbs up. I give her two thumbs up in return.

3

Lucia greets me immediately as I come into the dayroom. She's bright and cheerful.

"Good morning, Dr. Poser."

"Good morning, Lucia."

She asks me if I remember the cleaning lady she married in the past life. I ask her to tell me about it.

"I married her; I don't know if she married me."

Then she begins chanting, over and over: "The boys with the boys, the girls with the girls; the boys with the boys, the girls with the girls . . ."

She shows, with her hand, a diminutive figure, as though demonstrating the height of a child: "My mother's like that, like an angel."

We sit down.

"Dr. Poser, you know you look like God, but don't tell anyone; you'll get in trouble . . . Thinking about life in the womb . . . going back to 5, 4, 3, 2, 1. . . ." Then she shuts off completely from talking to me and begins praying softly to herself, hands together, eyes closed, steady rocking from the waist. After about five minutes, she gets up and walks across the room to another chair, crosses herself, and resumes praying. She starts talking to herself.

"I'm a boy, not a girl; I'm a boy, not a girl . . . They cut off my bottom in the hospital . . . eleven months, that's how long it took me, so the hands and feet came out okay; there there, sweetheart, it's all right . . ."

Leaving the dayroom at the end of the day, I run into her again.

"You look so nice, Dr. Poser," she says, noticing the handkerchief in my jacket pocket.

She gets a beatific smile. She leans her head toward me as though to nestle it into my breast, opens her arms to embrace me. She touches my shoulders softly with both hands. I can't bring myself to prevent her. I make strong eye contact, give her a quick but strong embrace, then let her go.

"Thank you for talking with me, Lucia," I say. "I'll see you next week."

She sits down and resumes praying softly to herself.

4

Lucia is pacing the dayroom talking to herself. I go sit by the window. She passes me. She's taking inventory: as she passes each patient she says, "baby." As she passes me, she says, "doctor, professor writing." Then she says, "They're already dead. I'm already dead. What more could happen?" She sits down in a chair a short distance away from me and begins praying. I put my hands together. She immediately notices and makes eye contact.

"Are you a priest?"

I don't say anything, just keep my hands together and maintain the eye contact.

"You say silent prayers," she says. "I can't say silent prayers; it would give me a heart attack."

She keeps watching me and begins giggling in a bizarrely forced way. She goes off and disappears into the bathroom. She comes out and heads straight toward me. She stands directly in front of me and asks if I'm an obstetrician-gynecologist.

"Why do you ask?"

She says that she's going to have a baby and wants me to deliver it. She urges me to come into the bathroom with her to deliver the baby.

"He's in my body. Take him out of me."

I ask her whether I can do it from where I am. She accepts this. She's very excited. She tells me that boys can have babies, too. She goes into the bathroom. When she comes back, she says, "It's yours. No papers to sign. I have enough babies. Thank you. Congratulations. Do you like little girls? I love girls. It's your baby. You gave me that baby."

5

The patients are going outside for a ten-minute break. Lucia's sitting, talking to something invisible on her lap. She's stroking it very tenderly, like it's a baby. The aide pressures her to get up. She resists, finally puts it down softly on the chair and continues to stroke it.

"There, there," she says. "Look, she's got stitches all over her face."

The aide leads her out of the dayroom. I meet her in the corridor when she comes back. She puts her hand on her belly.

"My mother," she says. "I redid her twice. She's just a little baby. But watch out when she gets the knife! She'll plunge it right in!" She points to her breast.

"Was that who was on the chair with you before?"

"That was my father. He's dead. I redid him once, but he died. I wanted them to come live here. Think of all the fun we'd have! Just like it used to be."

6

"I had my birthday last week. I'm thirty-eight."

"Happy birthday."

"Thank you."

"How was it?"

She stops talking and just stares at me.

"At my parents' house?" She starts crying. "I'm a dead body that never got buried. . . . I'm a little girl, not a little boy . . ." She repeats this over and over, weeping. "Why didn't they understand? . . . I redid them three times; they come in different forms now. When they're little babies, I look down"—she looks down—"when they're growing, I look here"—she points to waist height—"when they're grown up, I look up." She looks up. "I had my period. I'm a little girl. He suffered so much at the end. All right, honey, all right. Bye." We sit together in silence.

7

I'm talking with Lucia in the corridor.

"I'm shy with girls," she says. "I'm a boy but I look like a girl."

Then she gets upset: "I wasn't ever born to her. I wasn't ever in the womb."

She goes on into the dayroom. I go in after her, drifting over to where she has taken the chair in the corner.

"Can I sit down?"

"I'm not married to you. Don't mix me up with my sister. I'm a girl. She died a long time ago. I know. I know. You can make a baby by putting a boy with a man."

She stops talking and stares at my face.

"I'm so sorry about what happened to you. You've got bandages all over your face—here, here, here, and here." She points to her forehead, both cheeks, and her nose. "You have to put some medicated compresses on each of those places. Show me that you know where to put them."

I point to my forehead, both cheeks, and my nose: "Here, here, here, and here."

She looks carefully at my face and seems satisfied.

"I have to be going soon, Lucia. I'll be back next week."

"OK, Dr. Poser. Be careful."

I get up to leave the ward. Lucia closes her eyes and starts talking to herself. "All little babies, all my babies . . . I'm so afraid to claim them. The mothers and fathers come to claim them. They're looking for the same packaging pattern . . . My kids are all over. All right. All right. Dr. Poser takes care of them." Now she's talking to an invisible hallucinated version of me standing near her chair: "Dr. Poser. Hi. It's all right. Don't cry."

8

There's a quiet, meditative atmosphere in the dayroom. I'm sitting with Lucia in silence. After a while she starts talking.

"I'd like to have the key to the house where I used to live, but not yet, not until I'm an old lady."

"Tell me about it."

During the course of this recounting, tears begin streaming down her face, but they have no apparent connection to her tone of voice or the content of what she is describing.

"We lived on Cornelia Street. Very pretty. Lots of trees. You could walk over to where the Italian bakery and the cheese store was. My school was right around the corner. Our house was in a four-story brownstone, you know, with stairs going up to all the floors. There was a deli on the ground floor. They made the most delicious manicotti, ravioli, eggplant parmigiana. My grandmother lived on the second floor and we lived on the third. We had a dining room with a chandelier. There was a green velvet sofa and a big TV in the living room. My parents had the big bedroom and I slept in the little one. There was a little garden in the back and my father grew tomatoes but they never did much. There was a plum tree back there and it made some little purple plums at the end of the summer. I loved those plums. We never had to lock the back door because no one would ever think of breaking in. One time, I came back to the house with a big bag of groceries and got lost. They had to look for me in the street . . ."

This is the most coherent monologue I have ever heard from her. After her last sentence trails off, she stops talking. She seems absorbed in thought. I just sit with her. The tears have continued streaming down her face. After a few minutes, she says, "Thank you," and quietly walks away, taking a seat on the other side of the room, where she sits with eyes closed, softly crooning to herself. I stay where she left me.

When it's time for me to leave, I get up to say goodbye to her. I go over to where she's sitting. She looks up.

"Studying up on Freud?"

"That's an idea."

"I do remember something from when I was in school. It's a dog eat dog world. Can little children understand it?"

"Better than anyone."

"You're right, you're right. . . . A long time ago . . . I know all the . . . I can't get it straight . . . something might be there to kill you . . . you're doing very well . . . thank you."

"We do a little at a time."

"Right, right."

She smiles and walks off.

9

Lucia comes into the dayroom with the other patients who have been outside for a smoking break.

"Dr. Poser, are you the court jester for the gods? How's the transplant? I won't bother you. I'm going to confession. I was a boy anyway. It was just flap, flap, flap . . . big as a horse down there. All right, honey, . . . I know . . ."

She then turns around and drifts back across the room, talking to herself.

"All right, honey, they said only one more day. Animals in my arms. Skin, bones, sew it up and put a cast on it. When I'm ready to die, walk the kids home. Took me ages to learn that. Somebody's got to do it. Go to school. I see you, Dr. Poser. The court jester . . ."

The whole room becomes a cacophony of unrelated voices, wailing, and laughter. I just sit there writing in my notebook. Mrs. Lutzky comes up to me.

"Better watch your airplane. There's something wrong with your speedometer. You'll run out of gas. Those airplanes are antiquated."

She drifts off. Lucia comes back from her meandering. She's talking very fast, hitting herself in the head with her fist.

"I'm better. It was a hormonal imbalance. I'm in girls' ward. I'm not gay. I'm not a gay man. I'm happy. You're the court jester. You know what that means?"

"What does it mean?"

"What are those things you wind up and it jumps out?"

"You mean a Jack-in-the-Box?"

"Yeah. You wind it up and it pops out and tells the gods what's happening. It's very holy when that happens."

She turns around and drifts off again. I put my hands together in prayer.

"Don't make fun of me! You don't know what my problem is!"

"I want to talk to you."

"I don't want to talk."

"I thought we were friends."

"Yes, we are friends, but don't jump the gun."

I get up and go to the opposite end of the dayroom, near the exit. She remains in her chair, talking to herself. She repeats the phrase "Two dollars every three days . . . two dollars every three days . . ." over and over, then comes over to where I'm sitting and kisses me on the cheek. She starts singing:

"*But when I kissed a cop down on 34th and Vine / he broke my little bottle of / Love Potion Number 9.* You know that song?"

"Yes, I do."

"Dr. Hefner. Dr. Potatohead."

"Lucia, I never want you to feel that I'm making fun of you. It was an error and I apologize."

"I was in a bad mood. It's hard being here sometimes."

"It's a job, a job and a half."

"Yeah."

"I admire you, Lucia."

"I admire you, Dr. Poser."

10

The dayroom is chaotic; everyone is doing something—rocking, sleeping, screaming, or talking to herself. I'm sitting at a folding card table near the entrance.

Lucia is sitting cross-legged on the floor, singing quietly to herself. Agnes is sitting in a chair holding herself, waggling her foot and rocking back and forth, talking nonstop in her high-pitched, infantile squeal. Deborah, a newly admitted patient wearing a pastel ski parka, gloves, and a wool knit cap, is stalking through the dayroom, climbing on and off the windowsills, chairs, and benches, shaking her fists and screaming, "I'm a nice Jewish girl walking down the street! You want a punch in the face?"

Nicole is wandering around in a trance in her white nightgown clutching a scruffy old teddy bear.

Mrs. Lutzky is ordering Chinese food out of the air: "China Bowl Restaurant? I'd like to order in some food for the girls. They're starving us up here! They feed us garbage! What?? Bill it to Red China! Okay. Shrimp sweet and pungent, shrimp in lobster sauce, shrimp lo mein, beef lo mein, pork lo mein, five egg rolls, ten dim sum, you better make it ten egg rolls, Rice-a-roni, Chinese spare ribs, Stovetop dressing with roast beef, Rice-a-roni, I hope it's fresh, big spare ribs, duck sauce, a barbecued chicken, two barbecued chickens, you could freeze it, London broil, sirloin steak, rib steak, yogurt, you got any small children at home? fortune cookies, shrimp chow mein, pork chow mein, roast pork, won ton soup. . . ."

Lucia remains sitting on the floor, oblivious to all of this. Through the din, her sweet melodic voice rises like an angel. She sings: "*Silent night, Holy night / All is calm, all is bright / Round yon virgin, Mother and child / Holy infant so tender and mild / Sleep in heavenly peace / Sleep in heavenly peace . . .*"

Finally, the room seems to be quieting down. Lucia gets up and comes over.

"Did you have a hot date?"

"With who?"

She sits down at the table with me.

"Dressing up . . . it cost a fortune . . . My mother had a biopsy. Negative, thank God . . . a hernia, my father wasn't paying attention to it . . . male, men, hernia . . . when they get dressed and go out in the morning, they look like men . . . women look like boys . . . that's normal, isn't it?"

"Isn't it?"

She stares at me intently.

"What are you thinking?" I ask her.

"I'm thinking how beautiful you are. . . . I ate four cheeseburgers from the vending machines. I was so hungry, I ate them without putting them in the machine."

"You like pizza?"

"Yes."

"We should get you a whole pizza, all for yourself, with mozzarella and tomato sauce."

"That'll be our date," she says.

"I'd like that," I reply.

"Thank you."

She gets up, shakes my hand, and goes off.

11

Outside the building. Lucia is sitting by herself at a wooden picnic table. She looks withdrawn, absorbed in reflection. Across the driveway there's a hot dog vendor with his cart. I go sit down with her.

"You're very quiet."

"They doubled my Clozaril . . . Doctor Poser, will you buy me a hot dog? It'll be our date."

"You're on."

She gets up and we start walking toward the hot dog vendor.

"It's OK," she says, "it's a book. . . . Can I get mustard and sauerkraut on it?"

"You can get what you want."

She orders a hotdog with mustard and sauerkraut and a Coke. When she gets it, she immediately offers me half.

"No, thank you, Lucia; it's for you."

"How can I thank you?"

"Just keep talking."

She nods and we go back to the picnic table. She sits down and eats her hot dog and drinks her Coke in silence. After a while, she starts talking again.

"It's simple; something's not working in my brain. I won't betray you."

"I won't betray you."

"I was your mother-in-law. Did you have enough to eat and drink in the womb?"

"Never enough."

"You like to eat and drink a lot. OK. Do you have enough money? See you later."

She takes my hand and kisses it.

"Don't cry," she says.

She starts crying.

"What's upsetting you?"

"They put the wrong name on my honor card."

Tears roll down her cheeks.

"What would you like me to call you?"

"Lucia. . . . You remind me of my father . . . My mother is in the mental hospital, both my parents. It's three o'clock. When are you going home?"

"Soon."

"Do you mind if I go inside and see what's going on?"

"Not at all."

She gets up and goes back inside the building.

12

The nurse tells me that Lucia has had a seizure. We go into another room together where she has passed out seated at a table. She's slumped over with her head resting on her hands, drooling. She makes no response to the nurse's attempts to rouse her and seems totally unconscious. After several minutes of the nurse's continuous talking to her and stroking her head, back, and arms, her eyelids flutter. In a dazed, small, matter of fact voice, she says, "I had a seizure." With the nurse's help, I get her up on her feet and walk her around, holding her hand. We leave the room holding hands. She's still in a daze, but steady on her feet, like a small child who has just been awakened in the middle of the night. We sit down together.

"My name is Lucia, not Lucy—only my mother and father call me Lucy."

"What would you like me to call you?"

"Lucia."

She looks at me silently for a minute.

"You have a beautiful soul," she says.

"You have a beautiful soul yourself."

"You healed me. . . . Death be not proud."

She's quiet for another minute, then starts talking again.

"You know, I've been here for a long time. I had a mental breakdown my first year in college. I tried going home once but I ended up back in the hospital again. I've been in one place or another ever since.

I've seen Dr. Klein, Dr. Gross, Dr. Sullivan, Dr. Solomon, Dr. Ping, Dr. Pong . . . They say I've got schizophrenia. They put me on every drug there is. Then they keep raising them. Too much, I think."

"What helps?"

"Maybe prison."

She stops talking and we sit quietly together. After a while, she says, "Thank you . . . I see everything."

13

I hear thunder and go outside to look at the weather. The humidity is very high. It's just starting to rain. Lucia's coming in from sitting on a bench, smoking.

"Hi, Doctor Poser."

"Are you going inside already? What about going under the tree? It's cool and dry over there."

"OK."

We go sit on a bench under the tree. There's another woman on the bench, smoking a cigarette. Lucia wants one. She asks me if I think she can have one.

"Why don't you ask?"

She asks and the woman takes out her pack and gives her one. Lucia gets a light, says, "Thank you," and settles back to smoke it. We're quiet. I'm thinking about my daughter in Chicago.

"Thinking about your little girl?"

"Yes I was; how did you know?"

"You told me."

I have never mentioned to her anything about having a daughter, nor anything else about my family, for that matter. I get an uncanny feeling that she's reading my mind.

Then she says something about "crib death." Then she starts telling me about her parents. "They're aging gracefully; they're incompatible— he loves to work and she loves to keep house."

"Sounds like a pretty good arrangement to me."

We're quiet again.

She asks for my notebook and writes: "July 27, Dear Doctor, Thank you for being my friend. I owe you 25+25+25=75¢. You can charge it on the bill, please and thank you, Dr. Poser. So far, so good in Treatment Plan school. Summer vacation came and I'm out of school virtually except for a few classes. Love and kisses, Lucia Alighieri."

The other woman on the bench has remained quietly sitting there the whole time. Now she takes out three cigarettes from her pack and gives them to Lucia as a gift. The woman says she's a volunteer in the wardrobe shop and invites Lucia to come and get a new outfit for the summer. Lucia tells the woman she's Italian, Jewish, and Irish. I ask her if she knows any Dante. "Alighieri," she replies, and begins reciting in Italian. Then she starts hallucinating, gets up and intensely studies the ground, looking for something. She turns to the woman and asks, "Are you married to Doctor Poser?" The woman smiles and tells her that she's married, but not to Doctor Poser, to someone else. Lucia turns to me and says it's time to go upstairs now. She takes my hand and we walk up the stairs and into the front of the building. Walking down the entrance corridor, she introduces me to the front desk security monitor as her father.

"This is my father, he's a doctor."

Then she starts crying on my shoulder. I take her back to the ward. She's unwilling to give up my hand. She wants to continue talking. She asks me if I have a car. She wants me to take her to the Baby Zoo. I tell her I'd love to take her to the Baby Zoo.

We sit down. She's looking at me very closely.

"We look alike. I look like you and you look like me. You're my brother! No wonder I'm so attracted to you!"

"We're brother and sister."

"No, brother and brother."

Silence for a minute.

"What's wrong with me? Am I retarded?"

"No, you are not retarded."

"Will you be my doctor?"

"I feel like I already am."

"Can I get better?"

"Would you like to try?"

"Is there a school?"

"You're already in it; it's learning to talk."

"We do a little at a time."

"Yes, we do a little at a time."

I tell her it's time for us to stop now. She leans over as though to kiss me. I get up. All of a sudden, she panics. She bursts into tears.

"I'm scared! I don't want to stay here for the rest of my life!"

She gets up and presses her head against my chest and holds me with both arms. I give her a quick but strong embrace and then disengage. The therapy aide scolds her for getting a little too "lovey-dovey." Lucia withdraws back to her chair. She's still crying.

"Don't cry," she says to me.

I tell her I'll see her next week and leave the dayroom.

14

Lucia is plodding up and down the corridor, her arms slightly raised and gesturing. She's constantly speaking into the air. When I come through the doorway, she confronts me with shadowboxing movements.

"Are you going to take a slug at me?"

"I don't want to hurt you. I'm only fooling. I'm a prisoner—a prisoner of war. I owe you seventy-five cents."

"When you can afford it."

"You're the cuckoo doctor."

She goes to the therapy aide and asks for the two dollars allowance she receives each day. She gets it. She comes back and gives me a dollar.

"Thank you," I say. I give her the change.

"Is your leg still hurting you?"

"No, it's fine."

As a matter of fact, I had broken my ankle a year ago, before I came to the hospital, but it's completely healed. I have no idea what gave her the idea my leg had been hurting me.

"Did you have polio as a child?" she asks.

"No, that was my father."

This is true—my father had polio as a child, which left him with permanent weakness in his arms and legs and life-long problems with his back, neck, and shoulders. I feel at this moment as though she can see right into me. It's the second time in two weeks that I have felt this with her.

"Yes, yes, it's inherited"; she continues, "he had a full head of hair."

"That's right."

This is also true.

"You're lighter; you get it from the other side of the family. You take after your grandfather . . . Grandpa Giovanni."

She's right about all of this except for my grandfather's name. I'm stunned.

I give her my notebook. She takes it and writes: "Lucia Alighieri loves you. Always in my heart, always in my memory."

We sit together in silence.

15

Lucia passes me in the corridor.

"I don't bother you," she says, barely looking at me, then: "Remember what I told you: on the wave of consciousness, on the wave of consciousness."

I continue on into the dayroom and sit down by the windows. She comes and sits down next to me. I say nothing. I feel she's quite comfortable sitting quietly in silence. After a while, I offer her my notebook and pen. She takes them and begins writing. She's writing for quite a while. Finally, she hands them back. I thank her. I read:

"Dear Doctor Poser, I love you so much for even thinking of me. Consideration is so very important and so there is a doctor's degree for you. *Valley of the Dolls* by Jacqueline Suzanne is a book to be read, for change of your pills. How much of that book is true, I still don't know. The blue pills are my clozapine. The orange pills are ferric oxide, my iron pill. Fer sulf [becomes illegible] and lithium is a [illegible]. Going to school a pressure on my brain, but nothing else. And so it seems you are my best bet in psychiatric care, insane nursing care, and reverse therapy. I'd try to get a job for you at St. Elizabeth's. You can make a home there, too. Sincerely yours, Lucia. Love and kisses, Lucia."

We continue sitting together in silence.

16

It's quiet. I go sit by myself at the table at the far end of the day-room. I hear Lucia's cheerful, happy voice: "Judy, hi! Judy, hi!"

Mrs. Lutzky: "A hundred needles of rot gut up my vagina!"

Lucia to herself, hallucinating: "I just noticed you there, honey . . . Aww, it's all right, just telling . . . making you laugh . . . I know . . . December 30 . . . kindergarten, little kids . . . You know all about it . . . I took a test . . . The boys come as cops, the girls come as Olive Oyl and Popeye . . ."

She comes over and sits down with me.

"Ever get a job in Saint Elizabeth's?"

"Not yet."

"I'm studying to be a patient nurse," she says, then looks at me very closely.

"You're five years old; you're a baby. You look like the Gerber Baby. I can see it."

"You're right."

17

The therapy aides are having a hard time keeping Nicole in the dayroom. She's wandering in and out, dressed in a long white nightgown and clutching a raggedy teddy bear. She doesn't utter a sound and makes no eye contact with anyone. I go over and intercept her, take her by the hand, walk her toward the windows, sit her down in a chair, and immediately get another chair and put her feet up on it. I sit down next to her. She's absolutely motionless, her mouth hanging open, her eyes glazed. I get very comfortable and decide not to move from this spot so long as she remains where she is. I adjust my breathing to hers, which is very slow, put my arm around the back of her chair and just sit there. Lucia comes in from smoking and sits down on my other side.

"Babysitting, Doctor Poser?"

"She needs to be quiet."

Helene comes over, stands in front of us and proceeds to have a shrieking tantrum. Lucia interrupts her.

"Helene, your mommy's all right, thank God, so far, everything's all right in your family."

"You're not the nurse here, Lucia," Helene retorts angrily, then goes on shrieking and drifts away.

"I can only help you out a little bit," says Lucia, then to me: "Everybody's so scared here they're turning white."

We get quiet again.

Lucia's staring at the floor outside the doorway to the bathroom near where we're sitting. Suddenly she bursts out laughing.

"Isn't that cute? He does his own little teddy bear act, with the honey."

Nicole hasn't moved the whole time. She's in a stupor, a thousand miles away from here at the bottom of the ocean. Lily comes limping out of the bathroom with her pants down to her ankles, the third time today. She just stands there leaning back and forth and talking to herself with a sweet babyish grin on her face. Lucia is watching her.

"Doesn't she look like Paul McCartney? All boys have blue eyes—some shade of blue; all girls have brown eyes, don't they, Doctor Poser?"

"I think so."

Lily's still standing there until a therapy aide see her and comes over and pulls her pants up. She limps off. All of a sudden, Lucia pulls her head back in through the neck of her sweater and sits with her head inside her sweater, arms folded on her lap. She stays inside there quietly for about ten minutes. Then she comes out.

"Where'd you go?"

"I went swimming. Asbury Park. It's beautiful there . . . I miss swimming."

She gets up and goes off.

18

Heading toward the parking lot, I see Lucia outside on a bench, smoking. I go over.

"Hi, Doctor Poser, how's your mother?"

"She's fine."

This is not altogether true. My mother has recently gone in for tests to determine the cause of some abdominal pain and bloating. I am, in fact, concerned about what they might find.

"Oh good, good. And your father?"

"He's gone."

"He's fine. I'll take them over for you. They're safe with me."

"Thank you."

"Be careful driving. They'll get you because of the looks. Don't sit in the car. Get in from behind."

"I will. See you next week, Lucia."

"All right, Doctor Poser."

19

Lucia's sleeping in a chair by the windows. I go over.

"Can I sit down here and rest for a while?" I say. "I won't disturb you."

"Yes, that's all right. Do you want to talk? No, you need to rest, go to sleep."

We sit together in silence. She's curled up with her eyes closed, her knees tucked up to her chest. After about ten minutes, she starts giggling to herself, then breaks into hilarious laughter.

"How's my fella? Still three months old? Just about."

She starts laughing and gets up. She takes a few steps toward the bathroom, still laughing, turns and grabs her crotch with both hands.

"I'm bleeding so much! Having your period, second day. Usually I get it six or seven days. If I get it less than that I thank God."

Nicole is sitting by the door into the dayroom, weeping. Huge, agonizing sobs are coming out of her, the most audible sounds I have heard in more than six weeks.

Lucia goes over to her.

"Don't cry, it's all right, little Nicole. Hey, young lady, it's all right."

She goes over and holds Nicole's head in her hands and kisses her. Nicole's still sobbing. Lucia goes back to her chair and sits holding one hand on top of her own head. Then she addresses me from across the room: "Could you talk to her, see why Nicole's crying?"

"You tell me."

"Seeing funny things, feeling funny things, maybe her mother's told her she can't go back home."

20

Lucia walks by, talking to herself.

"Daddy, Daddy, Mommy, Mommy, Daddy with Mommy, Lucia with Daddy, Lucia with Mommy, Uncle Lucia, right, right . . ."

A therapy aide interrupts her and tells her she's not wearing a bra, that she shouldn't go around jiggling like that because some of the men downstairs are very fresh. Lucia comes over to me: "Doctor, will you get me a bra? I don't know what size. 36A? 36B? Get it for Christmas. I'll put my name on it."

Then she backs off and makes shadowboxing movements at me.

"I'm gonna get you," she says, then starts laughing, puts down her fists, and makes a circle with her thumb and forefinger. "I don't want to ruin your holy halo," she says. She goes off to the far corner of the dayroom. She picks up an orange and black soccer ball and starts tossing it up in the air and catching it. I go over, stop about ten feet away, and, without saying anything, put out my hands for her to toss the ball to me. She responds immediately, looks at me straight in the eye and throws the ball, overhand, first at my head, then at my crotch, then at my chest. Each time I catch the ball I toss it back to her underhand, very easy. Each time, she catches it and hurls it back at me. This goes on for about ten minutes. No words are spoken. Then, she simply holds up two fingers to signal that the game is over. She puts the ball down on the windowsill, says "Thank you," and waves to me.

From halfway across the room, she turns and waves back toward the ball on the windowsill.

A few minutes later, she's sitting on a couch in the middle of the room. Claire, another patient, comes over and lies down next to her. Lucia puts her hand very gently on Claire's head and strokes her hair.

As I'm leaving, she comes up to me.

"Did you get my son, baby Jesus? I left him in the hall for you. I'm still a virgin, it's the only baby I ever had, the Son of God."

"Thank you for telling me that."

"Every life is precious, precious. Me and Doctor Poser see everything, everything . . . Stay with her, Doctor Poser, I don't want to break up the marriage."

She smiles, turns and goes back to the couch to sit with Claire.

21

Lucia's in constant motion and talking continuously. She giggles as she passes me. This is some of what I hear:

". . . married too young . . . wanting to grow up . . . No honey, not yet . . . perforated clavicle, ovary . . . I hope my baby looks like my husband. . . . He's very, very dangerous about sex . . . All the babies have to look like him. I've got a plan . . . They came to this country again. They're going back to the old country. OK. The setting's always here . . . He's just nervous . . . picked on her for being a girl, he was really a boy . . . It was his parents . . . We may have to split it in the middle . . . going to peach, peach, . . . right, honey, right, right. . . . All right, little baby, all right . . . I kissed it. That was the boy baby . . . Geraldine Spreckles . . . My mother had no luck with girls . . . not too much . . . get sent back . . . boys . . . good little baby, good little baby . . ."

She's sitting down now, stroking her belly. After a while, she gets up and comes over to me.

"How much for the funeral?" she says.

She puts her head toward my shoulder. I say nothing. I'm stunned.

"You're sticking your neck out," she says.

"I know that," I reply.

The remark about the funeral, coming out of nowhere, completely shattered me. About a month ago, my mother was diagnosed with a suspicious lesion in her ovary. She's scheduled to go in for exploratory surgery in about two weeks. I've been preoccupied with this ever since her tests came back. I've cancelled my holiday trip to Europe just so I could see her through the surgery and take care of her when she comes home. Until this very moment, I had not allowed myself to even think it was possible that she might die.

22

A few days before Christmas. Lucia's talking to herself in the corner by the windows.

"... call the cops, ... how come you're so calm? I'm a piece of salami ..."

I go over, sit down, and give her my notebook and pen.

She writes:

"Have a Merry Christmas and a Happy New Year! Jingle Bells, Jingle Bells, Jingle all the way. Oh, what fun it is to ride in a one horse open sleigh. Dashing through the snow in a one horse open sleigh. Laughing through the snow in a one horse open sleigh. Lucia Alighieri."

She gives it back to me. I start humming "Jingle Bells" and we sing a few choruses together. Then she stops us.

"OK, Doctor, that's enough. I love you, Doctor."

"I love you, too, Lucia. Merry Christmas. I'll see you next week."

23

My mother passed away at Mount Sinai hospital of congestive heart failure the morning of my birthday, December 30. I hadn't seen it coming. My daughter Sophie had flown in from Chicago the day before to celebrate with me and to be with her grandmother. They adored each other. We went to see my mother in her private room in the hospital. She was funny and alert, but already being monitored for irregular heart symptoms. She told us to go out to dinner at a nice French restaurant for my birthday. She would see us both tomorrow. The hospital called me before dawn the next morning to say that she had passed away. This is my first day back on the ward following her funeral.

It's snowing outside. A therapy aide sits at a table near the entrance to the dayroom watching a soap opera on TV. I watch the TV with her. I'm very sleepy. I see Lucia curled up in a chair by the windows. She looks like she's asleep, eyes closed with clear saliva dripping from the corner of her mouth. I go over and sit down in the next chair. She never opens her eyes, never moves. We sit together like that for quite a while. The only sounds are coming from the TV, little snippets of sitcom dialogue and laugh tracks from the other side of the room. Finally, she breaks the silence.

"Do you feel safe?"

"Not exactly . . . You?"

"I'm playing with my toys in my dreams. It takes you to a certain place and not to others . . . certain places and not others . . . no fear, no."

We sit together again in silence.

24

Lucia gestures me over to her chair. I give her my notebook. She writes:

"Dear Doctor Poser, I love you so much and I always will. May be the smartest one in your class and may you graduate with honors! Find a good job somewhere in the doctoring field and you see how much that will lift your spirits. Good luck and always in my memories always in my heart is very very true. With much love, Lucia Alighieri."

All of a sudden there's a big commotion in the bathroom. There's some kind of fight going on.

Denise, a scrawny, boyish-looking woman, comes storming out, screaming. "They're trying to kill me! They're trying to kill me! Those fucking bastards! I hate those motherfuckers!"

She comes right past where I'm sitting with Lucia, takes off her shoes and throws them at me. Then she picks up a chair by the table and throws it onto the floor. The nurse comes into the dayroom.

Lucia, to Denise, in soothing tones: "Mommy loves you, Denise, don't worry. Don't worry, little girl." Now to the nurse: "Margie, get her a glass of punch."

The nurse goes off and brings back a paper cup with some juice for Denise. Denise calms down and goes off with the nurse.

Lucia turns to me.

"Are you OK?"

"I'm fine."

The dayroom gets quiet again.

"You know, Lucia, I'm going to be leaving in May, four months from now. I thought I'd better tell you."

She's quietly reflective, taking this in.

"I have lots of problems. I'll tell you before you leave."

"Thank you, Lucia."

"We do a little at a time."

25

Lucia is sitting at a folding card table by herself in the rear of the dayroom. She beckons me over.

"My parents came to visit. I just got back from lunch."

"How was it?"

"We had a picnic in the back of the car. Same as last time."

She gets quiet, then she starts counting in French. "*Un, deux, trois, quatre, cinq, six, sept, huit, neuf, dix, onze, douze* . . . What's thirteen?"

"*Treize.*"

"Right, right, *treize, quatorze, quinze, seize, dix-sept, dix-huit, dix-neuf, vingt, vingt et un* . . ."

She seems very pleased when she gets to a hundred. Then she starts counting in Italian. She stops counting and looks at me very directly.

"Can I ask you a question?"

"What do you want to know?"

"Why can't I go home to live with my mother and father?"

"That's a good question. What do you think?"

"I don't know, Doctor Poser. What does it say on my chart?"

"I don't look at the chart."

"It was fine when I was a little girl. I remember pushing a baby carriage with my little friend on Cornelia Street. We had Raggedy Ann and Raggedy Andy dolls and we pushed them in a carriage up and down the block. My grandmother lived on the second floor and we lived on the third."

"What was your grandmother's name?"

"Beatrice."

"That's a beautiful name, like in Dante."

"Alighieri . . . I miss my grandmother. My whole world came to an end when she died. . . . Is it because I got bad grades in school? Is that why I can't go home?"

"Lots of kids go through a time when they get lousy grades in school. It's not the end of the world."

"Am I too crazy? Is that why I can't go home to live with my father and mother?"

I say nothing.

"I *hate* it here!" she bursts out, then starts weeping, tears streaming down her face.

"It's okay to have feelings."

"Can I get better?"

"I don't know. It depends. It takes courage."

"Can I go home when I die? Will it be all right for me to go home when I die?"

I say nothing.

"I *hate* it here! I'm only forty-five years old! I don't think I can make it to sixty-five!"

Tears are streaming down her face.

"I've never seen you better than you are right now," I say.

"Go away and let me cry."

She puts her head down on her hands and starts bawling.

I get up and leave the room.

26

Lucia's been perambulating the dayroom for most of the morning, talking to herself and hallucinating. She stops and calls out to the nurse: "Nurse? May I tamper? May I tamper Pumpkin? She can't see or hear . . . kind of innocent, kind of retarded, mentally disturbed. . . . I'm Jewish, Italian, French . . ."

She passes me.

"Hi, Doctor Poser. Are you really leaving May 21?"

"Would you like to sit and talk?"

She sits down.

"Well, it's true. I am leaving the hospital in May. But it's only February. We'll have plenty of time before then. I'm thinking of making a pizza party, maybe outside by the gazebo if the weather is nice. It'll be springtime."

"Was that our honeymoon? Did we get into it, honey? Did I get pregnant? I must have."

I offer her my notebook and pen. She writes:

"Dear Doctor Poser, I love you so much and I love you! Please let me know if you need some money free of service. Good luck with your new job now and I hope you return here. Love you, Lucia Alighieri."

She gives back the notebook and pen, then starts talking about Hansel and Gretel. Their mother and father didn't want them at home any more. The witch was going to eat them, but they escaped. Then she raises her hands and repeats, "All gone! All gone! All gone! All gone!" like she's talking to a baby.

"I'm going out for a while, Lucia. I'll be back after lunch."

"OK, Doctor Poser, I'll be here."

27

Lucia comes to sit with me. We're looking at Claire, who is hobbling around the dayroom with her feet turned inward at the ankles.

"You know, Lucia, Claire told me that since I was here in a girls' ward, I must be a girlie, too."

"She doesn't know whether she's a girl herself. I have the same problem. I'm a little hairy for a girl, but I've got the right shape. I delivered three babies, two boys and a girl. My father helped me, but the little girl got burnt, burns all over her body. I took her to Mount Zion or Our Lady of the Andes—some hospital. How are the boys?"

"They're fine."

"Doctor Poser, am I married?"

"I don't know, Lucia, do you feel married?"

"Yes."

"To who?"

"I don't know, is it Nicole?"

I don't answer. We resume watching Claire hobbling around the room.

28

Downstairs in the vending machines area, Lucia is sitting on a couch holding two cans of soda, one in each hand. She holds one out to me.

"I want to give this to you from the bottom of my heart."

I hesitate.

"Please take it, I want you to have it."

I accept.

"Now we can go outside to smoke," she says.

We go through the security doors and out the front door of the building.

"I'm so sleepy; I don't know what hit me."

"Sometimes you just need to sleep."

She gets a light for her cigarette from another patient. We go to find a place to sit. The first benches outside the building are crowded with patients so we go further to an empty bench under a tree. There is still a light covering of snow on the ground. The sun is very pleasant. She takes deep, sucking drags on the cigarette.

"Spring's coming soon," I say.

"My parents came to visit last week."

"You're very lucky, you know."

"Yes, I know . . . and they all look like my mother. . . . I had a shower last night—I was a real mess."

"It feels good."

"You know what I need, Doctor Poser? A good stiff prick. I wouldn't tell the priest."

She chuckles, then lights her second cigarette off the end of the first one.

"I'm worried about the children. I'm not ready to take care of them . . . are you taking care of them for me?"

"You do things when you're ready. Meanwhile, they're safe with me."

We sit in silence for a while.

"My daughter's coming to visit me today," I say.

She gets a beatific expression on her face.

"I didn't know you had a daughter. How old is she? Twelve?"

"You'll be surprised; she's much older. She was just twenty-six."

"But you're only five."

"I was a baby when I had her."

"And what do you call her? . . . Sophie?"

This is, in fact, what I call my daughter, though I've never mentioned it to Lucia or anyone else in the hospital.

"How'd you know?"

"I saw it advertised on television. Sophie Poser—that's a nice name."

She finishes her second cigarette.

"Would you like to go inside now?" she asks.

"I've got to get something from my car. You go ahead."

She waves and goes off toward the building.

This is the third time Lucia has stunned me with what she is somehow able to see or know about my family. The first time was her telling me things about my father and grandfather, the second with the intimation of my mother's dying. When I came back to the ward after the funeral, sitting with Lucia in silence, I had the feeling, though no words were spoken, that she was nevertheless in communion with me, comforting me in my grieving. In every instance, I felt as though I were transparent to her, that she could see into my mind in some inexplicable, uncanny way.

Later that same day, I sit with her again. Again, we're watching Claire, who is now out in the middle of the room, cursing and threatening the therapy aides.

"It's no wonder you're feeling sleepy," I say; "if I were here, I'd be like you."

"No feelings, just be here."

I give her my notebook. She writes:

"Dr. Lucia Alighieri. wishes you well. I love you, Doctor Poser, it is ridiculous, as the best doctoring friend I ever did see or have. Love and kisses, XXX OOO XXX OOO, Lucia Alighieri, Dr. of Medicine and Psy. Medicine is right."

She gives the notebook back.

"You're a good doctor, Lucia, you helped me with Nicole when she was sick. We brought her back together."

"Maybe it's better some people rest in peace . . . nobody lasts here very long."

"You know better than I do."

"I think I'll go back to sleep now."

"Thank you for letting me sit with you. I'll see you next week."

"All right. Dr. Poser; say 'Hi' to Sophie."

29

Lucia greets me as she comes into the dayroom.

"Hi! . . . gorilla blood . . . How are you? Casting a spell on me?"

"Are you casting a spell on me?"

"I'm Merlin the magician. I'm Merlin the magician. I wish I had a magic wand."

I smile.

She goes off.

I spend most of the rest of the afternoon with Mrs. Lutzky.

At the end of the day, I go sit with Lucia.

"Are you getting married to Lutzky?"

"No."

"Are you in love with her?"

"No."

She holds her breasts in both hands.

"Doctor Poser, my breasts are tender."

"Are you having your period? That can sometimes be the reason."

"Come over here, I want to show you something."

She raises her blouse with both hands.

"Lucia, I'm afraid this isn't an exam room. Just sit down and talk to me."

She doesn't want to. I feel she's angry at me for all the attention I had given to Mrs. Lutzky.

30

Lucia says she wants to leave here and go to Saint Bartholomew's. She's afraid the drugs she's taking will give her a seizure. She says she wants electroshock—she had it once and snapped out of it. Then she starts hallucinating and talking to herself:

". . . never go to Saint Anthony's . . . this is your home. Daddy'll get you out of here . . . another year or two . . . It's all right, honey. All right. It's not bad . . . all the old people . . . I'm forty-four. I can't tell my past life . . . Car 54, where are you? I used to do that work . . . All right, honey, all right. Bye."

Then she starts talking to me:

"I don't know if I can ever go home again. I don't blame my parents. I blame chances of circumstances. You can't pick on chances of circumstance . . . You've got the same problem. Go home to your mother and father. You heal me, now I'm going to heal you. You know what I'm talking about."

31

It's Easter time, about six weeks before I'm meant to leave the hospital. Lucia's sitting on the floor, playing with some wooden blocks. She recites a magical formula, then gets fascinated with a stuffed Easter bunny in a little rocking chair that's sitting on a nearby table.

"Where'd that bunny come from?" I ask.

"From you," she says.

She starts singing: "*Here comes Peter Cottontail, hoppin' down the bunny trail, hippity hoppity, Easter's on its way . . .*"

She's making circles on the floor with her hand. She kisses herself on the shoulder.

"A pumpkin . . . a cake . . . with a big nose . . ."

She repeats the magical formula. She goes off to the bathroom. She comes back and resumes sitting cross-legged on the floor next to me.

"Are you comfortable?"

"Yes."

"Do you want anything from me?"

"No, that's all right."

Silence.

She starts giggling, talking to herself, more giggling. She presses her palms on the floor.

"I'm not making fun of her . . . all right . . . God bless you . . . all right . . . no one should beat me up . . . All right, honey . . . sure, sure, we didn't, all right . . . Hi, Natasha. . . ." She begins cooing. "Now, now . . . as you know, I have a vagina. Va-gi-na. I'm playing. All right, honey; all right, honey; all right."

She stretches out on the floor, hands at her sides, palms down, legs outstretched, eyes closed.

"I'm playing swimming, floating, no seizure, I'm playing . . ."

Suddenly, she sits up and turns to me:

"You heal me. . . . How's Sophie, . . . your daughter?"

She starts singing: "'*Smile, though your heart is aching, smile even though it's breaking . . .*' Doctor Poser . . . I know he's married . . . Sophie . . . all my babies . . . seventeen pounds, a bouncing baby boy . . . I like baby boys . . ."

She sits up, leans back against the radiator.

"I'm not having a seizure, Doctor."

"You're fine."

"I suffer all the little children to come unto me. Babies suffer. I know everything. When the baby can't go on any more, a switch goes off . . . do you understand? Nerves and cells take over."

She lies down full length on the floor again.

32

I go downstairs to the vending machines. Lucia's there. She wants to go outside. We sit down together on a bench. She's giggling hilariously.

"I'm hospitalized; did you know that?"

"Yes, I do know that."

"Are you really leaving May twenty-first?"

"Yes. I'm making a pizza party."

"A pizza party, right . . . You're as crazy as I am. . . . I'm going apple-picking at one o'clock."

"Where are you going to pick apples?"

"In a van."

She starts giggling again. After ten minutes, she excuses herself, gets up, and goes back inside the building.

33

Lucia is sitting by herself on a couch in the vending machines area. I ask her if I can sit with her. She gestures me to sit down.

"How's Sophie?"

"Fine."

"Do you think I should have shock treatment?"

"What do you think?"

"I worry about school a little, but I'm not really a worrier."

She's sniffling, then blows her nose in a tissue.

"Do you remember Saint Bartholomew's? I'm there now, transferred from Haddon House."

She sits quietly.

"Any visitors?" I ask.

"They didn't call."

"Let's see, when were they here last?"

"Do they still care about me?"

"Of course they do, do you doubt it?"

"No."

She falls silent.

I give her my notebook and pen. She writes: "Dear Dr. Poser, Have a great day, today and always. Much appreciation for the work you've been doing. Good luck on your new job in the future, and may God bless you and keep you forever more. Love and kisses, your friend, Lucia."

We go outside the building together. She tries to bum a cigarette from several patients and staff but doesn't succeed. We sit down on a bench. We're looking at the view across the hospital grounds, the lawn, the trees.

"Spring has sprung," I say.

She asks me where I live, what kind of a house I live in.

"It's not far away from here. If you can get your parents to bring you, you're welcome to come visit."

"That's OK, Doctor Poser. What time is it?"

"It's four o'clock."

"I have to be going back now."

She gets up and goes back into the building.

3 4

I go sit next to Lucia. She's wearing black tennis shoes, grey socks, bright pink stretch pants, a green sweatshirt, and a jacket. She looks like she's asleep. She opens her eyes and tells me she's going downstairs at one thirty. She's getting two cigarettes. She's sniffling. She says she's got a cold. She gets up to get a tissue to blow her nose. She comes back. She sits with her hands folded and her eyes closed. She coughs.

"Am I getting visitors today?"

"I'm here," I say, "is that OK?"

"Yes."

She starts giggling, then starts talking in a variety of voices—mother, baby, little girl. "I think it's pot roast, roast beef, Oh no, Ma! . . . I'm fine, I'm an angel. I'm in heaven. Wait 'til you get what Mommy's got . . . get to know your *real* mother. God knows where she came from. What's the worst that could happen? Gets up to heaven . . . See that? Even if you're bowlegged! What's that? What is that? I don't know. Do you believe in magic?"

She starts singing: "*Do you believe in magic? / In a young girl's heart / . . .*"

Then back to talking: "Don't forget, you're being nice to him. No help. All right, all right."

She's quiet for a while. Her hands are folded in her lap, her legs stretched out on a chair. She starts talking again:

"It's me, Lucia . . . I'd like to leave, Mommy . . . Sure you can leave . . . one, two, three, four, five, six, seven, eight, nine, ten, eleven, twelve, thirteen, fourteen. Spend it a little at a time. Lucia Alighieri—in the envelope. As if they did not know. As if they did not know. As if they did not know . . ."

She stops and stares into space, then says, "Are you all right, Doctor?"

"I'm fine."

"Sabbatical, two-year internship."

She gets up.

"Save my seat," she says, then goes across the room and into the bathroom.

She comes back and sits down one seat over, leaving a space between us. She's talking a mile a minute. ". . . He sees it and he writes it down. Doctor Poser, Steven Poser . . . can't sit there any more . . . you're going to have a baby . . . I'll get nervous. I'll get excited. All right, Mom. Try a hospital for you. Mental institution is better . . . a child's first memory. I'm better. I'm feeling better. Doctor, you're driving me crazy!"

"I am?"

She giggles.

"Don't ever think you're hurting me," she says. Now she's in tears and bawling. She gets up, goes to the bathroom, and comes back.

"Please leave me alone; I've had enough," she says.

I get up and leave.

35

This is my last regular full day on the ward. I see Lucia sitting at an outdoor picnic table, her head resting on her hands folded on the table. I sit down quietly on the opposite side. She looks up. "Hi, Doctor Poser," she says, sleepily.

"Are you having a nap? I don't want to disturb you."

"No, it's fine."

It's very mild. The air is sweet. We sit quietly without speaking. After a while, she asks me to take her to the cafeteria in the rehab building and buy her a hot dog. I agree. We go over. They unlock the building for us. She orders a hot dog, then turns to ask me if she can have sauerkraut and mustard on it.

"Get what you want."

"Thank you, Doctor Poser."

She gets the hot dog and a Diet Pepsi and we go back outside. She sits down at another picnic table and proceeds to eat the hot dog in four or five bites. Some sauerkraut falls on the ground and she gets concerned about making a mess. I tell her that some birds will probably find it. She gets under the table and rubs the sauerkraut away. We walk back toward the main building. She tells me about a male patient who touches her breasts and bothers her whenever he sees her. She doesn't like it.

"Thank God he doesn't touch me on the bottom."

"Do you know how to tell him to leave you alone when you don't want company? Same way you do with me when you don't want me bothering you."

"Yes."

She stops and turns to me.

"I'm going to miss you."

She leans her head toward me until it's resting on my chest.

"I'm going to miss you, too."

We go into the building together.

36

The last day. It's a beautiful morning in the middle of May. When I first come in, I see Lucia sitting on a couch downstairs in the vending machines area. She's drinking a soda. I ask whether I can sit with her.

"Share my tortures with me, . . . I look like a clown."

She's wearing a red blouse and turquoise stretch pants.

"I'm having my period; I have a heavy flow . . . blood clots. It means I'm very fertile . . . my fertile years . . . you're married, right, Doctor Poser?"

I say nothing. She starts talking about her birthday.

"What was your favorite birthday?"

"The first, I'm alive."

She looks at me in a peculiar way, then turns her eyes toward the corridor.

"What was that?" I ask her.

"I just saw my father go by in the hall."

She pauses, then continues. "You know, when I was a little girl I rode a white horse on the carousel in the Luxembourg Gardens. Round and round. Music was playing. I fell off the horse trying to put a wooden stick through the brass ring. I hurt my knee . . . Don't cry, sweetheart, there, there, don't cry little girl. . . ."

We sit quietly together. She's drinking her soda. After a while, she gets up and goes back upstairs to the ward.

37

It's time for the party. The therapy aide announces that we're all going outside now for pizza and that everyone should line up in the corridor. We escort them to the elevator. It's broken. We have to take the stairs, three flights down. Outside in the courtyard, there's a large open-air gazebo with benches and tables inside. Most of the patients sit down. Dr. Hartman, the director of psychology, and several other staff people join us. The delivery man from Lombardi's is waiting in a Jeep. He's got twelve pizzas packed in two large insulated carriers. We've also got a dozen liter bottles of soda in assorted flavors. All this gets set up on tables just outside the gazebo. When everything's ready, the patients start passing by the picnic tables and dig in. There's not much talk. They get their food and eat it. I'm standing around talking to various patients and staff people. While I'm busy saying goodbye to several of the other patients, I see Lucia go off by herself. She's heading off along the side of the building. I don't know how I'm going to say goodbye to her. The therapy aides have all gone inside after the patients. Everybody's gone. I go around to the parking lot. Lucia might be sitting out in front of the building. She's free to stay outside until four o'clock. I tell myself I'm going to get in the car and just cruise once around the front of the building to see if she's there. I start the car. The oldies station on the radio comes on. It's the Moody Blues: "*We've already said 'Goodbye' / Since you've got to go / Oh you'd better go now / Go now Go now Go now / Before you see me cry / I don't want you to tell me / Just what you intend to do now / 'Cause how many times do I have to tell you / Darling, darling, / I'm still in love / With you now?"*

That settles it.

I drive myself out for the last time.

Credits